W9-BJR-894

Additional praise for WORKING FROM THE HEART

"What a gift . . . WORKING FROM THE HEART reminds us that we don't have to compromise our ideals and values when we choose our vocations, but can instead learn how to employ and enhance them."
Audrey DeLaMartre, Minneapolis

"Wouldn't it be wonderful to have a wise and loving Mentor to guide us through the emotional, intellectual, and spiritual 'thickets' that keep us from finding joy and meaning in our Work? If you happen to find such a real-live being, you're very lucky; meanwhile, WORKING FROM THE HEART strives to fill the gap by showing how we can BE that Mentor for ourselves and for each other. It's obvious that this guide is presented out of a deep caring, compassion, and respect for humankind."
Yana Parker, author of *Damn Good Resumé Guide*

"At last! A do-it-yourself guide for people who want their work lives to be an expression of their best selves . . . A wise, caring and heartening book. WORKING FROM THE HEART goes beyond career development; it is a gift to anyone who wants to live more fully."
Tom Dunne, Organization Development Consultant and Career Counselor

"As a high school teacher in an affluent suburb, I find in today's graduating seniors a disheartening tendency to think of careers primarily as a means of having a BMW in the driveway and possession of other material luxuries. WORKING FROM THE HEART provides a thoughtful and practical program to help young people choose career training or select college programs that they will need in order to make a life and not just make a living."
John Heins, high school English Teacher, Virginia

"The ever-present hope of this book is inspiring, a mix of idealism and practicality."
Loret M. Ruppe, Former Peace Corps Director

Working From the Heart

For those who hunger for meaning and satisfaction in their work

by Jacqueline McMakin with Sonya Dyer

San Diego, California

LuraMedia ™

Cover Design by Carol Jeanotilla, Denver, Colorado

LuraMedia
7060 Miramar Road, Suite 104
San Diego, CA 92121

Library of Congress Cataloging-in-Publication Data
McMakin, Jacqueline.
  Working from the heart : for those who hunger for meaning and satisfaction in their work / by Jacqueline McMakin with Sonya Dyer.
     p. cm.
  Includes bibliographical references.
  Includes index.
    ISBN 0-931055-65-2
    1. Vocational guidance—Handbooks, manuals, etc. 2. Vocational interests—Handbooks, manuals, etc. 3. Job satisfaction—Handbooks, manuals, etc. I. Dyer, Sonya. II. Title.
HF5381.M3965   1989
650.14—dc20

89-12821
CIP

ACKNOWLEDGMENTS

Many people had a hand in shaping and supporting the production of this book. Tish Kashani, one of our seminar participants and our first administrative associate, said, "If only I had learned these tools in college, what a difference it would have made!" Her enthusiasm and helpful research skills got us started. Tom McMakin, Jackie's son, then in college, asked us to work with his friends and urged us to write for a broad audience. He had major input on the final drafts. Friend and colleague Rhoda Nary helped shape the first draft. The title was suggested by Barbara Liles. Critique and input was contributed by Jean Peterson, Peter Bankson, and Mary Claire Powell. Elizabeth Conant has believed in our work and offered invaluable support all along. Our present administrative associate, Melissa Stricker, nailed down technical details. Last minute help was offered by Judy Funderburk, Sally Dowling, Ricci Waters, Susan and Alison Hogan.

Our husbands, Dave McMakin and Manning Dyer, endured the whole process with good spirits and continual support. Our other children, Peg McMakin, and Larry, Nancy, and Barbara Dyer, all lived the vocational issues we were describing and provided insight and examples, as did our seminar participants and friends, whose impressive commitment to the challenge of finding meaningful work sparks our own.

Special thanks also to Lura Jane Geiger, Marcia Broucek, Lenore Thomson, and Jan Daugherty from LuraMedia.

CONTENTS

I think most of us are looking for a calling, not a job. Most of us, like the assembly line worker, have jobs that are too small for our spirit. Jobs are not big enough for people.

Nora Watson
interviewed by Studs Terkel in
Working[1]

Introduction: How to Use This Book

Do you believe there is something more to life than earning enough for adequate food and shelter? Have you ever wished that your work made more of a difference in the world? Are you willing to invest the time and energy necessary to find work that really satisfies?

Our world cries out for motivated and gifted individuals who will seek workable, imaginative solutions to the problems that confront us. Our communities need the support of people whose work — because it is needed, well done, and comes from deep within the center of themselves — produces an atmosphere of possibility and purpose. Do you want to be this type of person? Do you want:

- To have a calling that is large enough for your spirit?
- To see meaning in your labor beyond the reward of a monthly check?
- To see your abilities recognized and valued?
- To view yourself as a craftsperson, creating something of beauty and value?
- To feel you are leaving the world better than you found it?

If so, you are one of many people deciding not simply to hold down a job, but to work from the heart.

Across the land, there's plenty of work to be done — kids to be taught with care and creativity, cities to be restored to top working order, safe efficient cars to be built and maintained with integrity.

There's work to be done. And what is needed is work well done — accomplished with spirit, imagination, and commitment. Yet thousands of people are drifting vocationally, discouraged from finding work that satisfies or alienated from the work they have. This book will help you to think in depth about:

- What **GIFTS** do I want to use in work?

- What gives my life **MEANING** and how can I incorporate that in my vocation?

- How do the **PRACTICAL PARAMETERS** of my present life shape my vocational choices?

- What **VOCATIONAL FOCUS** do I want to choose and how will I explore it?

- Who will be my **COMPANIONS** in my quest for meaningful work?

- What ongoing **NOURISHMENT** do I need to discover and sustain work from the heart?

- How can my **WORK ENVIRONMENT** foster work from the heart?

- What is my **NEXT MOVE**?

Each of these "key questions" forms the basis for a chapter. Each chapter, in turn, is divided into seven numbered segments — if you like, one for each day in the week. Six of the segments include:

a reading for reflection

suggested activities

These are designed to be completed in about a half hour. Because each segment is brief, you will have time to reflect on the material and allow it to root.

In each chapter, the first five segments prepare you for the sixth, which is a group or partnering session, called Gathering.

Gathering session

The activities in this sixth segment can be done with one or more like-minded people who want to help each other find meaningful work. Generally, they will take about an hour and a half altogether.

The seventh segment of each chapter will help you to integrate the experiences, information, and ideas generated by working through the chapter as a whole.

Throughout the book you will meet people from our seminars and others we know about (with names changed) who have successfully wrestled with the questions the book raises. Their experiences will illuminate your own. You are in good company.

To decide how you will use this book, recognize and value your present situation. Then respond to these questions:

- **Will I simply read the book?**
  You'll receive much.

- **Will I do the activities?**
  You'll receive more.

- **Will I find a partner to use the book with me?**
  You'll receive even more.

- **Will I form a small group with which to use the book?**
  If you are a person who likes group interaction,
  this approach can be an especially rich one.

If you are planning to read the book without trying the activities, go with what attracts you. Some parts of the book may appeal more than others. Let your inclinations lead you.

Tips For Doing the Activities

Make space. If something new is going to happen in your life — a new awareness, a different kind of work, a fresh way to do the work you now have — you'll need to make room for it to grow. This is partly a matter of setting aside a special time and place for thinking and dreaming and doing the activities.

- Make appointments with yourself; reserve times in your days and weeks to do the suggested activities.
- Set aside a particular place in your office or at home where you can read, write, and ponder.

Assemble your materials. Decide right now whether you prefer to record your discoveries in a notebook or on 3" x 5" cards. It is easiest to record your thoughts and drawings in a journal or notebook, and some activities do presume notepaper of some sort. You may, however, wish to record specific gifts, talents, or ideas on separate 3" x 5" cards and put them into a file box. The advantage to this approach is that you can arrange your information in different sequences as your outlook changes. You might also choose to get a binder form of notebook so that you can take the pages out of different sections and look at them together. Once you've decided, obtain your materials, plus some pencils and pens (colored felt-tips might contribute to your creativity), and keep them reserved especially for this work.

Cultivate an expectant spirit. You're attracted by the idea of working from the heart. This means that you intend something to happen. Let it.

Bring your playful and serious sides to this effort. A combination of commitment and lightness releases creativity. Recent brain research points to new ways of liberating creativity by using both sides of the brain: the left side, logical, linear, and rationally oriented; and the right side, where feelings reside, images prevail, and fantasy abounds. The activities in the book encourage both left- and right-brain involvement.

Some suggestions may strike you as odd, or even downright foolish. They aren't. They are intended to help you listen on deeper levels, to get down below the conscious, rational, left-brain level, and by doing so, to tap inner sources that are visual rather than verbal. To find work from the heart, every part of you — the child, the clown, the mystic, as well as the planner and thinker — must be fully engaged.

Organize your materials. Get tabs for your notebook and/or filebox so you can arrange the discoveries you make in categories. The easiest way to do this is to use the chapter topics for category names. For each chapter, create a Summary Page. Use the designs suggested on the next page or make up your own. On these Summary Pages you will enter your most current insights as they occur to you. Use pencil for this so you can readily modify your entries as new insights come.

Pointers for Working with a Partner or Group

Gather kindred souls. Talk to people about your interest in finding work from the heart. You may be surprised by the number of kindred seekers who would like to join you in a disciplined quest. Talk with neighbors, work colleagues, and friends. Invite them to join you. You'll find at least one like-minded partner.

Be clear about specifics. Using this book involves:
- 8 Gathering sessions,
- 1-1/2 hours per session,
- 2-1/2 hours to prepare for the session (the preceding five 1/2-hour individual activities),
- commitment to attend each session.

Suggested Chapter Summary Page Designs

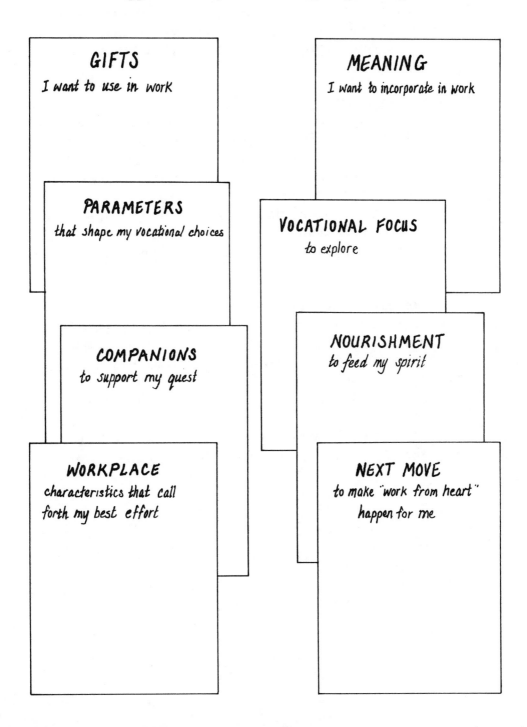

GIFTS
I want to use in work

MEANING
I want to incorporate in work

PARAMETERS
that shape my vocational choices

VOCATIONAL FOCUS
to explore

COMPANIONS
to support my quest

NOURISHMENT
to feed my spirit

WORKPLACE
characteristics that call
forth my best effort

NEXT MOVE
to make "work from heart"
happen for me

Decide how many people to include. You may prefer to work with one other person or to gather a group. The main thing to look for is energy and commitment. It's better to have one person who is as motivated as you are about this quest than four others who are not sure about it.

Decide on logistics.
- *Location of sessions:* A home is usually conducive to a cohesive group. If you do need to meet in an institutional setting, try to find a spot that is quiet and comfortable.
- *Time:* Choose a time that works best for everyone so that absences will be minimal.
- *Dates:* Set dates for all 8 sessions at once and agree to plan around them. This is always a challenge for busy people. Grit your teeth and take the time to do it. You'll be glad you did.

Decide on leadership responsibilities. If you are partnering, the two of you should share responsibility for leadership. Groups should decide whether leadership will be rotated or whether the same person or people will convene the group for each session. Here's what the leader or leaders do:
- Look over the Gathering session and collect the necessary materials.
- Work out a schedule for each part of the activity suggested. Consider posting the schedule on newsprint, so that each group member can agree to it, and help the group as a whole to stay on track.
- Start the meeting and outline the agenda.
- If necessary (depending on the size of the group), move the group through the activities, keeping to the agreed-upon timing.
- Help the group to formulate a modified schedule if there are reasons to alter the schedule mid-stream.

Even though you have designated leaders, everyone needs to help the group go. Don't sit back. Share, listen, encourage. Help keep the agreed upon focus and together the group will move forward.

Agree on some ground rules.

To build momentum and encourage each other, commit to these simple understandings:

- Make all Gatherings a priority. Plan around them so you don't miss meetings.
- If you need to be absent, let someone know.
- Be on time. If you have an unavoidable delay, let someone know if possible.
- End on time, or agree when you will end.
- Do the individual activities and readings between Gatherings and come prepared to give and receive.
- Bring all your work to each session.

Make your meetings lively.

The following suggestions work well to keep things flowing and fruitful. Consider reading them aloud before each session and reminding each other of them when needed.

- Share what is fresh for you as a result of doing the individual work.
- Don't get bogged down with opinions.
- Engage with each other — say a little, let others engage with you. Don't run on forever.
- Share what's most important. Do some sifting.

Remember — the purpose of the Gathering sessions is to stimulate you to go back to your individual work (where the real pay dirt is) with new gusto. So it is not always necessary to finish a discussion or complete a thought. Research shows that unfinished tasks keep creativity going and brain cells churning. So if your allotted time for a certain activity is up, leave it undone and move on.

These suggestions for getting the most from the use of this book come from 20 years of experience in a variety of individual and group settings. They are open to your modification as you develop your own best work style; however, each idea is worthy of reflective consideration so that the issues it seeks to address are not forgotten.

**Important as the "how to's" are —
most important is to begin.**

Doing What You Love

The question is not "Do I have the gifts and strengths that I need for my life?" [but] "Am I seeking to discover my gifts and strengths?"

Paula Ripple
Growing Strong at Broken Places[1]

A Field Guide to Your Gifts

Ninety-one-year-old Malcolm has a flair for color and a knack for carving. Paints, wood, marbles, and glue jam the kitchen in his small home. All year long Malcolm produces handmade toys for the school kids in his county for one reason: "I like to make children happy." Intricate doll furniture, tricky puzzles, colorful wagons, and — best of all — conversations with grateful boys and girls crowd his busy days.

"I work until I get tired or hungry," he says. "Then I stop just long enough to take a nap or eat something and I start again."

Sarah's excellent service in the paint store where she works tells you how much she enjoys what she does. She knows her product, cares about her customers, and takes great pleasure in seeing the freshly decorated homes and buildings that result from her efforts. Sarah is hospitable — she makes you feel welcome. Her forthright personality and direct approach help you clarify what you need and find what you want. You get the sense that Sarah has found her calling; she's in the right place.

Malcolm and Sarah are fortunate. They know what they love to do and have found a way to do that at work. That's what gives them such deep satisfaction. They offer to others their particular gifts of personality, knowledge, and skill through the tasks they do every day. Their experiences direct us to the first question to address in our quest for meaningful work:

What gifts do I want to use in work?

Addressing this question involves two tasks: first, *naming* the gifts you have; second, *identifying the gifts* you want to use in work.

Let's look at these two tasks in more detail.

If you think of gifts as "something you're good at," you might have the common reaction, "I'm not sure what my gifts are or even if I have any." Let go, for the moment, of that first instinctive definition. Think instead about the *"activities you love"* — perhaps being alone in the woods, appreciating fine craft work, wrestling with the kids.

Are the "activities you love" really gifts? Sure! Either they are gifts or they point to them. Wrestling with the kids, for example, could mean that athletic ability is one of your talents, or maybe it points to another gift — rapport with children.

A gift can also be a *personal characteristic.* On the PTA committee where they serve, George sparks the group with enthusiasm and buoyancy, whereas Jan tends to be cautious, asking thoughtful questions when a decision has to be made. Both George's enthusiasm and Jan's caution are gifts.

Used more broadly, the term "gifts" also includes *personal experience* — good or bad. Harry's heart operations were hardly what anyone would call a gift. However, once a week you can find Harry, now recovered, visiting patients in the hospital as part of its "Mended Hearts" program. He knows what these people are going through because he has been there himself. In a very real sense, his own experience with surgery is a gift he can offer others.

Having a gift does not necessarily mean you have skill or talent. Jessica has fond memories of singing around the family piano as a child. Now she wants to help her own family enjoy music. She doesn't play an instrument, has never had formal musical training, and, in truth, does not have much musical ability. Rather, her gift is love of music. This she passes on to her family.

Using this broad view of gifts, you can see that each of us has a bundle of skills, loves, characteristics, and experiences that are special to us. That is what is meant by the term "unique gifts." Uncovering and naming your particular gifts is the first step toward discovering the sort of work that will make full use of what you can offer.

Once you've named your unique gifts, the next task is to identify which of these you want to use in work. All your gifts need not be employed vocationally. Some may be better used in avocational pursuits. For example, if you have great rapport with kids, you may not want to use it on the job, but rather in off-hours as a Scout leader.

Before going any further, you need to be alert to perhaps the most dangerous obstacle you will face in your pursuit of work that fits your heart: *false humility.* This is the stone to be rolled away from the proverbial tomb housing new life. Many of us have been taught that blowing our own trumpet is "bad," that to speak of one's gifts is precocious in youth and pretentious in adulthood.

This is probably true when chatting it up at parties but is nonsense when you're on the road to discovering meaningful work. Identifying, developing, and offering your gifts is the way the work of the world best gets done.

Gifts are like muscles: The more you use them, the stronger they become. Your ability expands and you grow as a person. The opposite is true as well. Unused gifts, like unexercised muscles, lose their power.

When you do the kinds of things you like to do, and do well, the quality of your contribution to the world improves, thereby improving the quality of society. Research on stress shows how vital it is to your health to enjoy what you do. Employment studies demonstrate that motivated people enjoy their work and are more productive than are those who view employment as drudgery or duty.

Using your gifts has larger social ramifications as well. In two psychological studies, two office waiting rooms were each programmed with music interrupted by a news broadcast. The people in one room heard a human interest story of a positive nature. The people in the other waiting room were exposed to bad news.

In the first study, members of both groups were questioned about their view of humanity. Those who had been exposed to good news were upbeat, and their answers reflected optimism and a willingness to give others the benefit of the doubt. The unfortunate ones who had heard bad news thought much less of humankind.

In the second study, behavior was monitored. Those who had heard good news behaved more cooperatively with a stranger. The ones exposed to bad news were competitive and doubting toward a stranger.

The conclusion: Good news helps to produce positive feelings — and positive feelings tend to generate giving attitudes and behaviors. Bad news does the opposite.[2]

The relevance of this experiment to your quest? By engaging in work that fills you with satisfaction, you encourage the increase of good news in the world — the positive energy, the compassionate and just acts. *By doing what you love to do, doing it well, and taking joy in it, you can make a positive difference in the world.*

To help get you started in identifying your gifts, consider this slightly off-beat question. Write down your responses in your journal/notebook.

What would you be
if you could be something else?

Use your imagination. If you could be an animal, what animal would you be? If you could be a color, a car, a flower, a place — what would you be?

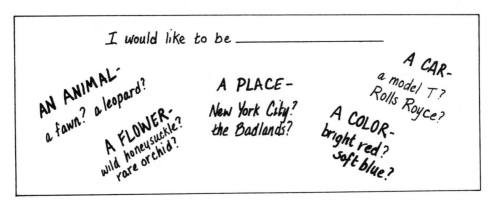

Now go back and ask yourself why you chose what you did. Reflect on what your choices tell you about special gifts you might have.

> Susan found herself thinking that she'd like to be a bright red Corvette convertible. Why? "I like red," she offered simply. "It's dynamic, fiery, full of life! And the Corvette is a true classic. I also like the idea of being open to the wind and weather." As she thought more about this, Susan realized that she was describing qualities that she liked in herself — her dynamism, her sense of freedom, even her "classiness."

Write down the names of the gifts you have discovered in doing this exercise.

2

We all need to do a lot of exploring and experimenting to define our gifts. Many of us think we are supposed to know all this when we leave school, or that there is nothing new to find out about our talents after that. Not so! Keep looking and listening . . . and don't ever stop.

Joan Smith Rideout
Sermon, Shrewsbury Community Church, Vermont[3]

You Are Your Own Best Expert

Sara Lightfoot, a professor at Harvard's Graduate School of Education, believes in the importance of letting individual gifts thrive. In an interview with Bill Moyers, Lightfoot expressed her commitment to enabling that process.

Moyers: How do we encourage children to recognize what they have to give in school?

Lightfoot: They need to be praised for individual expression, for the ways in which they are different from others and not always praised for the ways that they are like others. Kids are proud of their gifts. If they do something well when they're little, they announce it. They want praise for it. So it's not so hard to figure out how to get them to feel good about their gifts. But once we've told them that those gifts aren't appropriate or legitimate in the school environment, then it's very hard to rekindle that later on, and they'll stop bringing them there.[4]

School, family, and society tend to reinforce those gifts that are well-defined, predictable, and have acceptable outlets for expression. In the process, other, less well-defined gifts are squelched and remain undeveloped. However, you are still the best expert on what you really love to do and be. Your hidden capacities aren't lost; they still exist in the creative, "right-brain," playful, childlike parts of yourself. You can tap this expert knowledge — if you can shut off your "left-brain" efforts to direct it into familiar and predictable categories and definitions. Don't work at the following activities. Have fun with them as you relocate the "child" within.

 Draw a simple sketch of yourself. Identify what you love doing with various parts of your body: head, ears, mouth, hands, legs, feet, heart, etc.

When John, one of our seminar participants, did this, he drew:

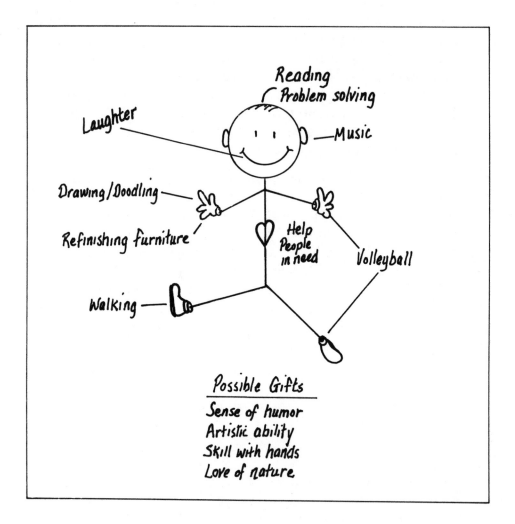

Look at your sketch and think about what gifts are involved in each activity. Write down each gift you identify.

Tapping into childhood memories can help you get in touch with long buried gifts. But accustomed ways of thinking and even daydreaming can actually serve to keep those gifts buried. In a sense, you need to bypass habitual modes of thought to "become" the child within. Allow yourself to experiment in this exercise with using your *nondominant* hand to do the writing. This will help you remember lesser known or forgotten parts of yourself.

Get a pencil and your notebook ready. Then take a moment to relax and be still inside. Sit back and remember what it was like to be 12 years old. As the sense of yourself at 12 takes hold, pick up your pencil and write your name with your nondominant hand. Then write a sentence as your 12-year-old self. Who are you? What are you like? Expand this sentence to a paragraph. Follow your hand, and let your mind speak from a different, perhaps more primitive, place than you do with ordinary conscious thinking.

Now take a look at what you've written. Switch your pencil to your dominant hand and continue writing about who you, as a 12-year-old, want to be when you "grow up."

Getting in touch with what you loved as a child may help you to rediscover some gifts that you have forgotten. Reflect on what you have written and list the gifts revealed through your trip back in time.

3

Helpful in dealing with our envy or jealousy is the knowledge that these feelings are giving us clear warning that we have abandoned ourselves . . . . Envy is a symptom of lack of appreciation of our own uniqueness and self-worth. Each of us has something to give that no one else has to give. When we can stay at home with ourselves and give what we have, we will not be threatened by what others have to give.

Elizabeth O'Connor
Eighth Day of Creation[5]

Looking at Yourself Through Green Eyes

Psychologists say that what we most admire in others can indicate a hidden or undeveloped gift in ourselves. When Jake, for example, remembered a woodworker he had met and admired in Kentucky, it helped him realize how much he loves beautiful crafts and working with his hands, particularly with natural materials.

The dark side of admiration is envy. It, too, can alert us to our own gifts, but it may take some probing to discover what in ourselves is seeking recognition. When Sally heard her friend Rhea complimented for her public speaking ability, she felt immediately envious. "What does this mean?" she mused. "Do I want to get up there and make speeches too? No, I can't see myself doing that. Maybe it's the fact that people are making such a fuss about Rhea. I wonder if I want a more public sort of role to play."

In point of fact, Sally does have a gift for leadership, but she had been expressing it behind the scenes as an effective leader of groups. Her envy of Rhea's greater visibility ultimately led her to consider a more public kind of leadership role. When nominated for the vice presidency of the Tenants Association, she knew she was ready for this public role and gladly accepted and ran.

It is not easy to go through the reflections that Sally did. Sometimes it takes a long time to reach clarity. And there are instances when envy and admiration indicate no more than a wish to possess someone else's gifts. That, too, needs to be accepted. The point is that it is worth probing feelings of admiration and envy to see what hidden capacities they may reveal in yourself.

What gifts or abilities do you admire or envy in your family, friends, public figures, etc.? What do these admired skills tell you about the gifts, talents, and skills you enjoy using? As ideas come to mind, list each discovery.

As Carol worked with this exercise, she thought about Eleanor Roosevelt, a woman she had always admired. "Let's see," she said, "*what* do I like about her? I know . . . she triumphed over limitation, could take a positive stand without being fanatic, was an advocate for the oppressed. Wow! These *are* traits that I like in myself, but I've never managed to make them part of what I do in the world."

Eric Hoffer tells a story about a Bavarian peasant woman who cared for him after his mother died and during the years that he was blind: "And this woman, this Martha took care of me. She was a big woman, with a small head. And this woman, this Martha, must have really loved me, because those eight years of blindness are in my mind as a happy time. I remember a lot of talk and laughter. I must have talked a great deal, because Martha used to say again and again, 'You remember you said this, you remember you said that . . .' She remembered everything I said, and all my life I've had the feeling that what I think and what I say are worth remembering. She gave me that . . ."

Elizabeth O'Connor
Eighth Day of Creation[6]

Compliments Count

Evaluation and/or feedback is a frequent part of life. Formal evaluation starts in school with report cards, continues with job or college recommendations, and carries over into job performance evaluations. But in our open society, informal feedback is common as well:

"You played a great game of tennis."
"You stated that thought so clearly."

Is it hard to accept such compliments with a simple, "Thank you"? How often are you tempted to reply with a statement that downplays your good points?

"Oh, that was luck, not skill."
"You can't really mean that."

Or worse, how often do you tend to dwell on the negative feedback you get and forget the positive? Compliments from others, if we can hear and accept them, give us valuable information about our gifts.

A teacher's compliment to Ralph stayed with him through his school years and later pointed to a skill he would use in work: "You are wonderful at organizing people to accomplish a task together." Ralph's grade in this teacher's class was not high, but those words of positive feedback fueled Ralph's pursuit of a career in politics.

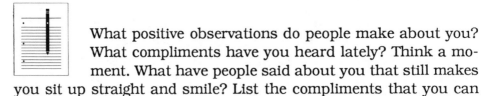

What positive observations do people make about you? What compliments have you heard lately? Think a moment. What have people said about you that still makes you sit up straight and smile? List the compliments that you can remember, and add a few words on how you feel about each. Then hazard a guess: What gifts do they suggest? Don't be bashful. Bask for a few minutes in the good stuff that has come your way.

5

This, I believe, is the great Western truth: that each of us is a completely unique creature and that, if we are ever to give any gift to the world, it will have to come out of our own experience and fulfillment of our own potentialities, not someone else's.
Joseph Campbell with Bill Moyers
The Power of Myth[7]

"Follow Your Bliss"

You've begun to name your gifts. Now it's time to take a more extensive look at the kinds of things that have given you deep satisfaction throughout your life.

In *The Power of Myth,* mythology scholar Joseph Campbell discusses with Bill Moyers the question of how to discover your life's purpose. "Follow your bliss," is his advice, " . . . go where your body and soul want to go. When you have the feeling, then stay with it, and don't let anyone throw you off."[8]

What exactly does Campbell mean by "following your bliss"? How do you know what makes you truly happy? Campbell says:

> The way to find out about your happiness is to keep your mind on those moments when you feel most happy, when you really are happy — not excited, not just thrilled, but deeply happy. This requires a little bit of self-analysis. What is it that makes you happy? Stay with it, no matter what people tell you. This is what I call "following your bliss."[9]

What is your "bliss"? Think about those moments when you have been "deeply happy," when you have felt you were really yourself, your best self — when you have felt most alive. These moments are "good experiences." Your good experiences may or may not have anything to do with work. And they have nothing to do with what others think, only with your own perception. Good experiences are the things that you have enjoyed doing, that have given you deep satisfaction — the things that you felt expressed "the real you."

If examples do not come readily to mind, don't work at coming up with something specific. Instead, be still, and make room for the impressions and wisps of thought that will come into your mind on their own. Remember *you* are the decider. Your good experiences are not necessarily experiences that have been recognized or valued by others.

Over time, make a list of 20 of your "good experiences." To do this, divide your life into four quarters, age-wise. For each quarter, list five good experiences:

Good Experiences in My Life

1st quarter (age   to   )

_____
_____
_____
_____
_____

2nd quarter (age   to   )

_____
_____
_____
_____
_____

3rd quarter (age to)

_____
_____
_____
_____
_____

4th quarter (age to)

_____
_____
_____
_____
_____

Here are four of the 20 good experiences that John listed (one for each quarter):

My Good Experiences

- concocting pranks at summer camp (age 8)

- regaining motor ability after sports accident (age 20)

- being a friend to my teenaged daughter (age 38)

- acting in the community theatre group (age 50)

This exercise is not easy for everyone to do. Listen to Laura's account of her process:

> "At first, I thought this would be easy. On the contrary, it was quite difficult. Not so much the earlier, childhood years or my twenties or early thirties. The real difficulty started with my middle years — my "barren" period, as I call it — where I not only stagnated but very nearly lost all my self-respect and self-confidence. However, several days later, after I had already finished this assignment, more and more past experiences surfaced to my consciousness and made me feel better even about those middle years. Nevertheless, I hope that I am on my way to an even better period and that I might be able to develop those hidden gifts which must be buried deep inside me."

Laura's remarks highlight several points about how to go about doing this. Give yourself enough time. Do it at one sitting if that is best for you. Or carry around a piece of paper in the car. Post the paper on the refrigerator or on your bedroom mirror so that you can jot down your good experiences whenever they occur to you. Or take a walk with no destination. Let your mind wander. Then sit and spin out your thoughts.

There may be some periods in your life where you find it easy to identify good experiences and other times in which it's hard, but do find some for each quarter, even if you have to consult someone who knew you during a particular period to jog your memory. Experiences in your early life, especially, can reveal parts of you that may have been lost or hidden as you grew up and took on more of the expectations of others.

GATHERING

Purpose: *To help each other discover and name gifts*
Leaders Bring: *newsprint, magic markers, pencils, paper*
Everyone Bring: *Good Experiences in My Life from Segment 5*

Warm-Up (Everyone)   **15 minutes**

Share with your partner or group one positive discovery about gifts that you have brought to this Gathering — either an insight from a reading or something you have learned about your own gifts.

Discover Gifts Together (Two's)   **60 minutes**

1. Work in pairs. Decide who will act first as Sharer and who will be the Listener.

2. The Sharer describes a favorite experience from the "Good Experiences in My Life."

    Let's use John's description as an example. He said:

    > "One of the things I put down was acting in the community theater group at age 50. When I hit the half-century mark, I wanted to do something special — something I had never done before. I had always wanted to try acting, so I signed up and plunged in. I'm getting a big kick out of it."

3. The Listener asks questions to help the Sharer elaborate. As the Sharer says more, the Listener writes notes about the gifts that he or she is noticing in the description.

    For example, Nancy served as Listener for John:

Nancy: John, why are you getting such a charge out of this?
John: Well, let me think. I guess it's that in my job, I have to be serious and on top of things most of the time. In plays I can act crazy. I love the bit parts and the character parts.
Nancy: What are some of the characters you've played?
John: I played a bum in one production. Then there was the nosy butler. One of the most enjoyable parts was an incompetent baseball player who was always striking out — a comic role — the fool, you know.
Nancy: What appealed to you in these roles?
John: All of these roles were, I guess, about little people of one sort or another — people who were not particularly talented or good at what they do — ordinary people muddling through. Now, let me see, what is appealing in that for me? Well, I guess part of me is these roles — I muddle through a lot but have to pretend too often that I really know what I'm doing. These roles seem real — authentic — and I like that.

---

4.   Repeat steps two and three as many times as possible within 20 minutes

5.   When 20 minutes are up, the Listener names the gifts that he or she has noted, gets the Sharer's response to the gifts just identified, and together they refine the list.

This is how Nancy and John worked out Step 5:

Nancy's Gift Identification for John	John's Response
John, seems like you have a great sense of humor. Is that right?	Yes. That's true. I love to see the funny side of things.
Willingness to try something new — that's a gift you must have.	Yes, I guess there is some of that in me.
Appreciation of ordinary people — their foibles.	Well, yes and no. I do like down-to-earth people, but not just their foibles. Their very real achievements. After all, these are the people who make the world really work.

6. Then the Listener writes a list of the gifts that both partners have recognized and gives it to the Sharer.

7. Reverse the process so that the Listener becomes the Sharer and the Sharer becomes the Listener. (Be sure to budget half your time for each person. It is disappointing if a disproportionate amount of time is used to name gifts for one person.)

How It Went (Everyone)   **10 minutes**

Pop-corn (a brief, easy, flowing sharing that builds on each person's offerings) how it was to be the Sharer and the Listener. Talk about what you learned and what you felt during the process.

Closing (Everyone)   **5 minutes**

Be sure to close the session in a way that creates a feeling of unity and completion, whether you are working in pairs or in a group.

IDEAS: Gather in a circle and share one or more of the following:
- words of appreciation for what happened
- ideas to make the next session more effective
- insights gained
- support needed for the next step
- a motivating reading or thought
- silence

NOTE: Subsequent Gathering sessions will include simply the word "Closing." Refer back to these suggestions if necessary. The point is to create a closing ritual that the group members or both partners feel good about.

A Greek neighbor used to lean over our mutual fence and say to me in her broken English, "Enjoy, enjoy!" She would close her eyes and tilt her head back to feel the sun on her face. She also said these words when she pointed to her amazing fig tree, sprawling in the corner of her yard where the fence met the house. Mrs. Loukas enjoyed life as a gift.

Mary R. Schramm
Gifts of Grace[10]

Enjoy! Enjoy!

The important thing is not how many gifts you have identified, but how much you enjoy using the gifts you have.

You may be delighted by your discoveries —

"Yes, that is a gift I have."

You will have some questions —

"How could this gift be incorporated in my work?"

You may have some doubts —

"Is this gift strong enough to be useful?"
"Is my gift as valuable as someone else's?"

All of these are common reactions. What matters is that you have begun the challenging, life-long work of gift discovery and have noted specific gifts.

Now it's time to sift and select those gifts you might want to use in future work. Remember that all gifts need not be used in work. Some are better offered in avocational pursuits — and others you may not want to use at all at this time.

Bill, for example, had spent much of his life crafting beautiful chairs and tables for a local furniture company. Now, with arthritis in his hands, woodworking is painful for him. However, his enthusiasm for the beautiful work his company turns out is still infectious. He is therefore cultivating that gift and retraining for work as a company salesman.

Bill's situation is quite straightforward. Cheryl's is not. At age 50 and in good health, Cheryl is seeking newness in her work life and, at this point, is asking questions. Having excelled at being a manager in a large corporation, she now wants to develop the artist in herself and is concentrating on painting to see if this is the right way to go.

What is your situation like? Ask yourself: Do I want to use the same skills I've always used but in a new kind of employment? Or do I want to use entirely different abilities in my work?

Add the gifts that your partner helped you name during the Gathering to the list of gifts you've already made. Now take a good look at all of them. Revel in what you have discovered. At this point, as you think about developing work from the heart, which gifts would you like to use on the job? Do some seem more alive for you than others? Perhaps you are tired of always using certain gifts. Give yourself a little time to look and reflect. Then star those that seem most important to include in your future work.

Write the names of these starred gifts on the Summary Page that you've created for this chapter in your notebook (see the Introduction, page xi). As you gather clues and fragments of information about yourself in this process, you will gradually develop a stronger image of yourself and what you want to do with your life. The Summary Pages will help you chart your progress visually as you move forward.

What's It All About?

Do you think they [our children] would believe us if we told them today, what we know to be true: That after the pride of obtaining a degree and, maybe later, another degree and after their first few love affairs, that after earning their first big title, their first shiny new car and traveling around the world for the first time and having had it all . . . they will discover that none of it counts unless they have something real and permanent to believe in.
Mario Cuomo, Governor of New York[1]

What Are You For?

Speaking at a high school commencement, New York's Governor Cuomo laid it on the line: Without some central motivating purpose, what we have and what we do has no meaning. Articulating this sense of purpose is one of the major challenges of existence.

The audience that Governor Cuomo chose for this message is significant — not a group of ministers or business executives on retreat, but high school students about to make their way into the world. This is when it begins — in high school: first a nagging feeling, then an insistent question, "What shall I do with my life?" and, finally, the even more basic question, "Why?"

Elsa, a graduating senior, summed it up well. "I know where I'm going to college," she said, "but I haven't the foggiest idea what I'm going to do with my life."

When asked at a graduation party in her honor, "Do you know where you're headed — what you'll do after college?" she replied simply, "I'm not sure yet." But later she admitted, "I wish that question were off limits. Does it really matter what I do? I can't make any sort of difference in the world, and what good would it do if I could?"

Underlying the question of how to invest her life lurks an ever-present temptation to despair over whether vocational choices matter at all. If you are honest with yourself, that question, and the temptation it brings, can reappear at any point in your life. The only antidote is a well-grounded sense of why life is worth living.

This chapter's key question has two dimensions:

What gives my life meaning and how can I incorporate that in my vocation?

It used to be that we could look to outside authorities to help us put together a package of meaning. The government, the church, or school pointed the way to purpose and vocation. Accepted bodies of knowledge and skill also filled that role: Learn the law, medicine, cabinetmaking, or masonry, and you will be a respected professional or tradesperson able to make a needed and valuable contribution to society.

Times have changed. No longer can we simply trust outside authorities to be our primary source of meaning. Events such as Watergate and the television evangelist scandals serve to erode the values we derive from the state and church. These institutions no longer are solely sufficient to support our personal experience of meaning and value. We must also look within and ask, "What makes sense to me, given my experience?"

In your attempts to do this, recognize that, at the very least, your point of departure will be other people's systems of meaning. You may even find, despite the alienation you sometimes feel toward your inherited past, that there are elements of value in those systems that you want to keep. The task at hand, then, is to springboard off your past into your own sense of meaning.

Assailed daily by headlines screaming about what's wrong with the world, it is easy to identify what you oppose. You know you feel sick about styrofoam cups littering once-pure rivers, or people unable to reach food supplies because of endless civil strife.

But what are you **for**? What if, like Martin Luther King, Jr., you were given your moment at the Lincoln Memorial to speak to your sisters and brothers about your dream for a better world? What would you say? More profoundly, where would you place your energy, your resources, your life? Create a short, imaginary speech that begins, "I have a dream . . . " In this form (or another that better suits you), write in your notebook a description of the world (nation, neighborhood, family, etc.) you want to help bring about.

2

To me, the evidence is overwhelming that we human beings (including your "opponent") are connected to one another in very real ways, that we're part of a common unity, as waves are part of the ocean. This view of reality is a remarkable source of guidance and staying power, particularly when you're dealing with seeming blackguards and the situation is really dicey.

John Graham
"Can Giraffes Survive in the Jungle?"[2]

Untying the Meaning Knot

Five years after Elsa's graduation party, she finished college. With her economics degree in hand and an increasingly strong desire to preserve the quality of our air, water, and land, she took a job with the Environmental Protection Agency in Washington, D.C.

"This is great," she thought. "It may be an entry-level job, but I'll be working for a cause I believe in."

One particularly blue Monday, having been on the job a year, Elsa found herself reflecting on the day ahead. She had come to dread going to work. "Sure I'm using my economics background and the cause is good, but the setbacks are so discouraging. Congress blocks our proposals, industry ducks enforcement efforts. So much needs to happen, but all we do is drag our feet. Why am I doing this another day? I hate my job!"

Elsa had values, interest, commitment — but something else was needed to sustain her through the difficulties. "I want a job with meaning, but if this isn't it, then what is?"

Meaning is *not* just a question of values — of what is important to us — but an interaction of world view *with* values. In other words, taking a job because you support a cause is like getting married because you want to settle down. The motive isn't fundamental enough to get you through the hard times and the disappointments. Naming your values and attempting to live them out will give you direction for a while, but it won't give you staying power in the hard tussle of everyday reality.

Contrast Elsa's experience with that of one of her colleagues, Andrea, who also works for the EPA — as a lawyer for the Superfund Project, which cleans up toxic waste. She says: "To me the universe is like an organism — a living, breathing whole. When one part hurts or is damaged, we all suffer. The health of one element strengthens the potential for health in another."

"I believe in life, I work for life," she continues. "I do what I can to preserve life. Sure, you're not always successful. But I'd no sooner stop trying than give up on the health of a small child."

Andrea would find it hard to believe that she had thought through a metaphysical and ethical stance toward life. But she has.

Meaning, for her, is the natural way her values — her life-nurturing compassion — flow from her view of the cosmos as a living organism. This sense of meaning in turn sustains her through the ups and downs of work.

All too often, questions of metaphysics and ethics are locked up in complicated text-book explanations and lost to ordinary awareness. Yet every day is packed with stories of how a world view joins values to create meaning.

Essentially, a world view is the fundamental belief undergirding the way you live your life — your philosophy of life. Values are your response to that world view; they are guideposts for your behavior. Meaning is the relationship between the two.

Although Elsa knew that she stood for a clean environment and found a job that had value for her, her position wasn't embedded in a philosophy of life that gave her work meaning.

A newspaper article on Desmond Tutu, the first Black Bishop of Johannesburg, contains these words:

> I pray for the [oppressive white minority South African] government by name every day. You see, if you take theology seriously, whether you like it or not, we are all members of a family — God's family. They are my brothers and my sisters too. I might not feel well disposed toward them, but I have to pray that God's spirit will move them.[3]

Let's break down this statement into the concepts just articulated:

World view: We are all members of the same family of God.

Values: Compassion and non-violence.

Meaning: Because we are all of one family, to reach out to the least likeable elements of society is to reach out to a sister or brother.

Or consider these words of Barb, a zoology professor:

> To me, evolution provides a powerful explanation for the way our world works. All species are primarily concerned for making the world safe for their babies. I have such respect for that life preserving force that the possibility of humans doing things to disrupt or damage that force is deeply offensive. I respect that force. I seek to understand it. I revel in it.

Like Bishop Tutu, Barb has a clear understanding of her world view, her values, and the way in which they interact to create meaning.

World view:	Life is an unfolding biological drama.
Values:	Respect, understanding, appreciation, and responsible stewardship.
Meaning:	Because I am but the latest manifestation of life, I have a responsibility to preserve and to honor it.

To talk about the dynamic and complex interplay between world view, values, and meaning in this way admittedly oversimplifies a phenomenon that defies rational explanation. Even so, in your attempt to articulate your fundamental beliefs, this scheme may be a useful lens through which to examine meaning in your own life and the lives of others.

Let's look at one more example of someone who is trying to be faithful to a fundamental belief system:

Jane works in a manufacturing plant. When her friends ask her why she wants to be the union liaison with management, she talks about mutuality, fairness, and harmonious relationships.

World view:	Human beings are created to work and live in harmony.
Values:	Fairness and mutual respect.
Meaning:	I want to build bridges between people who could easily be adversaries.

Jot down the names of two or three people who you feel have incorporated meaning in their work in ways that you respect. Write a short paragraph describing each, including, as best you can, their world view, values, and sense of meaning.

Then, treat them as your "meaning professors." Ask them any questions about meaning and work that are on your mind. Imagine what their responses might be. Write these responses down.

. . . Genuine meaning is never abstract, it is always personal. It is what moves us, stirs us, and leaves us transformed . . . . We live first; we reflect later. First, people need to articulate their own experience, then, to discern the unique pattern and unity that give their life meaning.

Brita L. Gill-Austern
"Awakening the Trusting Heart"[4]

Family Business

The family is an important source of meaning. Whether positive or negative, family experiences, attitudes, and expectations help form the vantage point from which you view the world and the way you choose to conduct yourself in it. If your family value system is to have power for you as an adult, it is helpful to think it out again from an adult perspective.

"Ours was a do-it-yourself family. We raised our own food and did most repairs ourselves," said Sandy, who was brought up in a small Tennessee farming community. Now he lives and works in a large city.

"My parents always said 'God helps those who help themselves.' I see the world as full of individuals striving to make a better life for themselves. As a result, I value self-reliance. My independence is clearly the product of my parents' world view."

Listen to how Desmond Tutu describes his mother:

My mother was hardly an important person at all in the way that South Africa and most of the world looks at things. She wasn't educated, but she was such a gentle and giving person that she had a powerful influence on me, not by saying anything but by just being herself. Leah [his wife] used to call my mother the "comforter of the afflicted." Any time there was a tiff between two people, she wouldn't say who was right. She would always side with the one who was getting the worst of it.[5]

No wonder her son's career often includes being a peacemaker in the midst of troubling conflict!

A variety of attitudes toward family heritage are necessary. Some portions of that heritage you may accept as valid for yourself, some you may respect, although you now take a different approach, and some you may wish to leave behind.

Make a family word collage. Include the occupations represented, places where you lived or your family lived, religious/philosophical viewpoints, cultural forces strong in the family, traits and attitudes you remember in some family members. You'll find as you're doing this that certain words lead naturally to others: Sandy, for example, naturally connected farming with Tennessee and the philosophy of self-reliance. The connections you make are part of your family heritage.

Look at each word in your collage. Circle those which represent something you believe in for yourself and want to express in your life. Cross out those which do not fit you. Here's Sandy's collage:

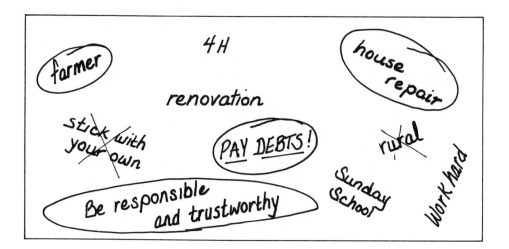

Next write a short statement describing important under-standings from your family which help shape your own sense of meaning. Again, here's what Sandy did:

> I want to work where my sense of self-reliance is valued. A small business, not a large company, is what makes sense to me. I also believe working with your hands is the most honest kind of work.

4

When you go around earth in an hour and a half, you begin to recognize that your identity is with that whole thing, and that makes a change . . . from where you see it, the thing is whole, and it's so beautiful. You wish you could take one person in each hand, one from each side in various conflicts, and say, "Look. Look at it from this perspective. Look at it! What's important?"

Russell Schweickart, lunar module pilot of the Apollo 9 mission
"No Frames, No Boundaries"[6]

Influential Life Experience

In the above quotation, Russell Schweickart describes the effect that his exposure to a radically different experience had on his world view and ultimately on his values. Many miles above the planet, completely free of the spacecraft, he truly felt the universe's mystery. If not changed, his conception of existence was powerfully expanded.

In turn, this world view informed the values he held dear. Suddenly several lengths out in front of other concerns — the desire to do well, to educate the next generation, to enjoy life — raced the concern to hold all life's activities in perspective. Suddenly the long view took precedence.

Whether hopeful or tragic, earth-shattering or relatively mundane, influential life experiences open us to deeper levels of meaning. Few of us will have the chance, like Schweickart, to break free of terrestrial bonds so dramatically, but many of us have broadened our horizons by changing location.

As a student, Ana majored in Spanish and spent time in Honduras polishing her language skills. There she fell in love with a Honduran man whom she later married. Living as a resident in that country for several years, Ana gained a deep respect for the culture and people, as well as a growing sense that people the world over share more in common than they realize. This way of looking at humanity — as one people — informed and reinforced Ana's drive (her value) to reach across boundaries.

Now, back in the United States, Ana is dedicated to communicating her love and knowledge of Hispanic culture to the students in her Spanish classes. Her firsthand, long-term exposure to another culture fueled her commitment to cross-cultural education.

Sometimes a sense of meaning can be traced not from a change of location but from a memorable experience in the past. Hal grew up in a small town in central Idaho. "We were all neighbors. Even if I didn't know someone, I knew they were friends of someone with whom I was friends. I was raised to think of the world as populated by neighbors, some close, some far, but all neighbors. For me, the man who ran the grocery exemplified this feeling. He knew everybody. I loved going to that store when I was a kid. He was such a friendly guy."

Today, years later, in a major eastern city, Hal still sees the world the same way and still lives the solid ethic it implies: neighborliness. At first it was hard for him — the big city seemed to laugh at his naïveté — but one day when he took a job as a Safeway checker things seemed to click into place. "I know that my job seems boring to some people," he says, "but I really love being part of people's everyday life. Shopping is such a drag for most folks; I like to pick up their spirits, make small talk about their families and all. I remember names and faces, and people feel good about that — about being part of a neighborhood where other people know you and enjoy seeing you. I often think about that friendly neighborhood grocer from my childhood; I like the idea that I can lend a little of that atmosphere to a huge supermarket."

The pain and grief of our lives can also contain clues to meaning. Brendan, stricken with cancer, came to know with new clarity what he had only vaguely felt all his life — that existence is a precious gift from God. Life is short; each moment is a treasure. Through prayer and writing, Brendan saw that this world view implied a very specific value for him: to pass the gift along.

He noticed that his doctors were uncomfortable talking with him about what it really felt like to be ill. The frustration and pain he experienced in that situation pushed him into a mission for the last weeks of his life. He decided to help physicians learn to talk to their dying patients with warmth and understanding. Inviting each doctor on the ward to spend some time with him, listening to his experience, he offered suggestions about the kind of personal sharing he thought other patients would appreciate.

Make a list of life experiences that have shaped your world view, inspired your values, and in turn rooted meaning in your life. Include any life-giving or life-affirming encounters you have had with the great philosophical or faith traditions. Also include, if you wish, any painful or difficult experiences that offer clues to meaning for you.

Look over your list. Select three of the most important experiences you listed. For each, find an object that symbolizes its importance for you. Assemble those objects and place them before you. Look at them and absorb the power of what they represent — a life-changing experience.

Then in writing, free associate about what these objects evoke in you. Try to be uncensored. Allow thoughts and feelings to surface at random and capture their aliveness. Don't worry about correct writing form.

5

In responding to vocation — the call, the summons of that which needs doing — we create and discover meaning, unique to each of us and always changing.

Marilyn Ferguson
The Aquarian Conspiracy[7]

Envision the Future

Recall Elsa's colleague, Andrea, who works as a lawyer for Superfund, the toxic waste cleanup project within the Environmental Protection Agency. Picture her on vacation the summer before she decided to work there.

At the water's edge, Andrea looked up the beach, out to the distant horizon, and finally to the sign posted rudely in the sand, reading "Closed." The reality of what that sign meant disgusted her. How could this be the same beach where she had spent her summers since childhood? Fresh flowers on the table from her mother's garden, long days swimming in clear ocean waters, hours spent gazing down at the teeming life that inhabited the tidal pools. Now this lovely stretch of New Jersey coast was closed. Three days earlier, hospital waste, including used syringes, had been found washed ashore. It was a crime. Andrea could feel the anger tighten in her throat.

Outraged, she knew what she wanted to do. At the end of that summer, she left the small Manhattan law firm that had hired her out of law school and assumed the position working on Superfund litigation. Employment in the toxic waste clean-up project was not always immediately satisfying, but there at least she felt as though she was part of society's best efforts to heal the earth's most open sores.

As the months have gone by and the heat of her initial passion has cooled, she speaks of being sustained by the fact that the work she has chosen to do is deeply meaningful. In a concrete way, her instinct to preserve life is given form. This value, in turn, both grows out of her conception of the earth as a living organism, and gives rise to a vision of the future for which she has commitment and passion — restore the earth to its pristine condition.

Any of the concepts already described — world view, values, meaning, and vision of the future — in and of themselves have little staying power. It is when they interact dynamically with each other and are rooted in significant life experience that they have power to move us.

Moreover, each of these abstract concepts resonates more with some people than with others. A strong sense of values might be the propelling force in one person's life, whereas a vision of the future might ignite another.

Outrage fueled a commitment in Andrea not simply to care for the earth, but to form a specific picture in her mind of what she wanted to work for and how she could do that concretely. Ana's experience of loving Honduran people and culture led her to work for cross-cultural understanding through teaching Spanish. Brendan's experience of anger, disappointment, and frustration during his hospital confinement moved him to change things for other people in his situation.

Passion, whether caused by fierce hope or profound discontent, can move us from the armchair into the streets. Passion points the way to compelling vision and meaningful action.

In Segment 1, you envisioned an ideal picture of the world you want to help create. You may have identified a whole grocery list of things that are important to you — craftmanship, peace, justice, neighborliness, clean environment, honesty, independence, etc. Consider now which of these you want to include in your work. What impassions you toward action?

Write your response to the key question of this chapter: **What gives my life meaning and how can I incorporate that in my vocation?**

GATHERING

6

Purpose: *To gain further clarity on the meaning and vision you want to incorporate in work*

Leaders Bring: *newsprint, masking tape, marking pencils, 10-foot length of string or yarn, 3" x 5" cards*

Everyone Bring:

Family collage and statement of meaning from Segment 3

Life experience descriptions from Segment 4

Response to key question from Segment 5

Warm-Up (Everyone)   **15 minutes**

Taking turns, stand up and assume the character of one of your influential family members.

1. Introduce yourself.
2. Describe some values you learned from your family.
3. Describe how these played out in "your" life. Have fun with your character. Exaggerate.

Support and Feedback (Three's)   **30 minutes**

1. Hand out newsprint and markers.
2. Each member: Draw a circle and divide it into thirds.
3. Spend some time drawing symbolic representations of each of your meaning-shaping life experiences (from Segment 4).
4. Show your drawing (to two others or to your partner) and share the thought that went into it.
5. Allow for questions and expressions of support.

Encouragement and Affirmation (Everyone)   30 minutes

1. Give each member a 3" x 5" card. (Partners take several.)
2. Use the string to form a small circle (about 3 feet across) on the floor or table. This is the wish pool. Sit around it.
3. Each member: Read your response to the key question (from Segment 5) to yourself. Then write a wish for the world on your card. (Partners write two or three wishes on separate cards.) Place the cards in the wish pool.
4. Spend several minutes silently reflecting on your wish.
5. Slowly, as the mood moves you, voice out loud your response to the key question. Allow space for each one to speak. When there is a feeling of summation, each person dips into the wish pool (partners each take half the cards), and then in a celebrating voice pronounces, "I wish for. . . (whatever is written on the card)."

Completion (Everyone)   10 minutes

Spend time discussing your feelings and insights about the session's reflection on meaning and vocation.

Closing (Everyone)   5 minutes

7

"Find the answer within yourself," my father replied, "for I tell you it is surely there."

Rita Reynolds-Gibbs and
Paula Underwood Spencer
"A Teacher's Guide to *Who Speaks for Wolf*"[8]

You're Not in Kansas Anymore

A Native American writer, Paula Underwood Spencer was taught her people's ways by her father. When she asked him questions, he usually replied with the response quoted above — the answer is within.

Most of us have not had that kind of encouragement to follow our own inclinations. Rather, the pressure has been to "follow the crowd," whether that crowd is our family, our church, our school, or our profession.

This chapter on meaning is about letting the "real you" stand up, speak out, and be heard. The questions posed are tough. Consider them over and over again from different angles. As you think about what gives life meaning for you, let your responses grow.

Open yourself to new input and a re-examination of what you have already received. Keep searching for a fuller grasp of what is needed in the world and how you can respond. The potter/poet/teacher Mary Caroline Richards writes: "I am a question-asker and a truth seeker. I do not have much in the way of status in my life, nor security. I have been on quest, as it were, from the beginning."[9] Her stance will serve you well.

Remember in "The Wizard of Oz," how Dorothy came to realize what home in Kansas meant to her only after she'd been over the rainbow? Sometimes you can't appreciate the gifts of meaning you've grown up with until you've left them behind and come back to them anew, from another vantage point.

Gloria understands this well. The liturgies and customs of the Catholic church had been a framework of meaning on which she had built her life and work. Then, gradually, without recognizing at first what was happening, she began to doubt, struggling with un-answered questions. It seemed to her sometimes that if her religious faith fell apart, what she cared about would lose its moorings and have no meaning. Her doubts lodged like a cold stone in her chest. More and more angry with her traditions's form and ritual, which no longer seemed to address her concerns, Gloria finally stopped at-tending church and began to think of religious faith as something she'd outgrown. Maturity, she decided, was to accept reality — to live without illusion.

Then a move to the southwest United States exposed her to Native American culture. Gradually a different kind of dance, art, poetry, and wisdom filled the gap left by her childhood faith. She felt her soul come alive. Initially, she thought that Native American ways of being and thinking had given her access to meaning that the church simply didn't recognize or welcome. Yet, over time, she felt a longing to return to church. When she finally did, she was surprised and moved to find that many of the rituals and customs that she had questioned did, in fact, intersect with what she had discovered in Native American expressions of faith.

Gloria says, "I go to church now because I want to be there, not because I am told I should be there. I bring my Native American wisdom with me. It's given me another way into the mysteries I didn't know how to accept."

Deepening one's perspective through exposure to new experience can be as dramatic as immersion in Native American customs or as simple as reading a magazine with a perspective different from yours. The important thing is to take a first step. Dorothy, as you recall, didn't decide to go to Oz. She was blown over the rainbow by a tornado. But the tornado overtook her because she had left the security of home. Gloria had no idea that she would enhance her sense of meaning through getting involved with Native Americans customs. But she was open to new experience and trusted what drew her. She did *something.* She went with what attracted her and was open to change.

Choose one or both of the following activities:

1) Resolve to expand your sense of meaning by seeing the familiar with fresh insight. A wise teacher once gave this suggestion to a student about to visit an art gallery: "Go through the whole exhibit rather quickly," she said. "Then find one painting that speaks

to you. Spend the rest of your time with that painting. Linger with it; let it engage you. Let your eye, heart, mind, and feelings relate to the painting. Savor it from different angles and distances. Do this, and you will have begun to probe the meaning of that painting."

Go on a personal treasure hunt. Note favorite objects, people, books, films. Select one that seems especially lively for you now. Then follow the teacher's suggestion: Linger with it. Let it engage you, etc. In this way probe the meaning it has for you and write it down.

2) Consider sources of meaning new to you. Open yourself to something you've wanted to try but never got around to doing. Experience a meditation period at a local Zen center. Spend a few minutes of quiet in a cathedral on your lunch hour. Move to music for a few minutes at home. Don't worry if you can't do something "big." Just do something. Draw a dream. Talk to someone who seems to be spiritually alive. Once you have done something concrete, take a few minutes to record your reflections, either in writing or by drawing in your notebook.

Review your work from Segment 5. Enter the main points on your Summary Page for this chapter.

3 Let's Get Practical

Meaningful work is important; so is a decent salary. Finding ways to bridge those frequently divergent paths may be one of the key quests of our generation.

Norman Boucher and
Laura Tennen
"In Search of Fulfillment"[1]

Narrowing Your Choices

So far you've only thought of hopes and dreams. However, untethered balloons are soon lost from sight and but a memory. In looking at the gifts you want to use and the meaning you want to express in work, you also need to ground your aspirations in reality. Don't groan. Reality can be refreshing. Your vocational choices are influenced not only by what you would love to do but also by what you *must* do to live the way you want or need to at this time. How those closest to you feel about what you do, your state of health, and your stage in life are additional factors that determine how much energy and time you have for future work, the money you need to earn, and the geographical location where you will work.

Limitation narrows choices. And that's not all bad. The key question of this chapter focuses on the impact of life's circumstances:

How do the practical parameters of my present life shape my vocational choices?

Simple to ask but tough to answer — because there are lots of ways to deal with limiting circumstances.

Take health. You might feel that nothing is so fixed and final as a physical disability. But look at Ted Kennedy, Jr. When he lost his leg to cancer, he was motivated to help others adjust to similar circumstances. A missing leg is a fixed condition, yes. But how you want that to influence your work is as flexible as you allow yourself to be.

Or money. You support a house and family and have a certain level of expense. That seems to be a given. But is it? Your kids and spouse might find it exciting to sell worldly possessions and follow you to one of the developing nations.

Practical parameters do influence work choices, but the form of that influence varies. Some parameters you must accept. That may feel like a limitation — and so it is; but a limit is not only a restriction. A limitation is also a priority that you are choosing to support. For example, if you say, "I can't do that because of my family," you may feel restricted by your conditions. The flip side of that limitation, however, is positive: "My family is a priority for me." Celebrate the integrity of your choice.

Other parameters are open to change. To find more time for family you might change from day to night-time work. To make more money, you might market your skills differently.

Taking the realities of your life seriously can be a great energizer. Newly divorced with three young children to raise, Nancy was at first overwhelmed. "I have to support the kids all by myself," she said. "How am I going to do that?" But gradually determining what she needed to earn, where she would live, and the kind of work she would like to do, she began serious job hunting and today is successful because she had to be. Necessity is the mother of adventure.

"I feel more confident, healthy, and vital than I have in a long time. I looked reality in the face and did what I had to do. The kids are doing well in school, we live in a cozy place, and I'm learning new things every day."

Parameters can also help in decision making. In this age of overchoice, it is helpful to know that some parameters are unchanging. "My spouse's job requires frequent moves, so I need work that is portable." That insight narrowed Beth's choices and helped her decide to get her real estate license so she could work anywhere in the country.

By the same token, lack of parameters can be disconcerting. "With Maria no longer here and my children not in the area, I can do pretty much what I want to do in retirement," says Bill. "But don't feel happy for me. I wish I had some constraints that would limit my choices a bit. Total freedom is really scary."

With no real limitations, Bill must rely on preference alone to guide his choices about what to do, where to live, and what satisfactions a job should deliver.

 To get a feel for how parameters influence vocational choice, think back to your own past. List four or five experiences of how practical parameters have shaped work choices you have made.

2

Carol chose. She wanted the promotion so much she could taste it. But the job came with weekends and evenings and traveling attached, and she didn't want to miss that time with her husband and sons. She couldn't do both. Knowing that didn't make it any easier.

Carol isn't the only one I know making these decisions. Another friend refused to move up a rung on the professional ladder because it would have meant uprooting his family and transferring his wife out of a career of her own. A third couple consciously put their careers on the back burner in order to spend time with the family they'd merged out of two previous marriages.

. . . The decisions they faced are the rock-bottom ones, the toughies. How do you divide the pie of your life — your own time and energy?

Ellen Goodman
Close to Home[2]

Reality Check

To understand how the circumstances of your life will affect your work from the heart, it is important to:

- identify your present parameters;
- choose the ones you want to change;
- take action to change them; and
- allow those you cannot change to help shape your choices.

You may find that there are more options available than you thought for dealing with the practical realities of your life. You may even discover that the parameters you thought of as restricting or limiting can be a source of energy and direction.

The following Practical Parameters Inventory considers the givens of your life — time, money, location, relationships, health, and age. **Check** the answers that most clearly mirror your own experience. If your situation is not described adequately, use the answer closest to your own circumstances as a springboard for a description of your own. Then **write** in your notebook or on cards answers to the Summary and Reaction questions at the end of each section.

If you, like Bill, lack practical parameters, go through the inventory anyhow, noting your preferences under each category.

PRACTICAL PARAMETERS INVENTORY

TIME

Time is a primary consideration in thinking about future work. You have already freed up time to explore and carry out your vocational search. As you think about future work, what are your time requirements?

How much time do I need or want to work?

- Full time
- Part time
- Other

What kind of work hours do I want to keep?

- Regular daytime hours
- Rotate schedule
- Night time
- Flex time
- Other

How will I balance other life priorities with work?

- I will build in specific time for myself each week.
- I will give priority time to relationships that are important to me.
- I will decide which specific activities outside of work I want to give time to.

Summary and Reaction:

- **What time parameters must my future work have?**

  (Summarize in writing the items you checked above. For example, "My future work must be full-time, weekday evenings.")

- **How do I feel about this?**

  (Record your feelings as accurately as you can now. They will fuel your answers to the next question. Know that feelings change. If you take this inventory another time, your feelings could be quite different.)

- **How will I respond to this reality?**

  (Note whether you want to change the parameter, change your attitude toward it, or whether you accept things the way they are.)

REWARDS

What constitutes reward is elusive. It can mean many things in addition to "putting bread on the table." It also includes level of responsibility, recognition by others, personal satisfaction, and the impact that you have on other people and situations.

What are my financial needs?

- I am the primary earner in my family and need substantial remuneration to support them.
- I am a secondary earner and need to make at least half of household expenses.
- Money is important as a symbol of being taken seriously.
- Money is not a primary consideration. I will go forward with my vocational choice regardless of what I earn.

How much do I want to earn?

- Above $30,000
- $20,000 - $30,000
- Below $20,000
- Other

How important are benefits?

- Major consideration
- Secondary consideration
- Not important
- Other

How much responsibility do I want?

- High level
- Medium level
- Low level
- Other

How much recognition do I require from others for what I do?

- Substantial
- Some
- Not necessary
- Other

How much personal satisfaction do I need from a job?

- I must love what I do.
- I must like what I do.
- I do not need to like what I do.
- Other

How much of an impact do I want to have?

- My work must affect many people and/or situations.
- My work must affect some people and/or situations.
- My work must affect a few people and/or situations.
- My work must affect someone.
- Other

Summary and Reaction:

- **What rewards should my future work provide?**
- **How do I feel about this?**
- **How will I respond to this reality?**

LOCATION

How do geographic considerations effect your decision making?

Is the location of my future work a limiting factor?

- My work must be in my present location.
- My work must be in my present location for now, but later on it can be someplace else.
- My work can be in any of the following locations:

  _____

  _____

  _____

- My work can be located anywhere.

- I am willing to travel.
- Other

How much of a commute can I tolerate?
- I want to be able to walk to work.
- Under 30 minutes
- 30 - 60 minutes
- Home on weekends only
- Other

Summary and Reaction:
- **What location features should my future work include?**
- **How do I feel about this?**
- **How will I respond to this reality?**

HEALTH AND AGE
Factors related to the health and age of yourself and those for whom you are responsible may influence your vocational choices.

The situation for me at present is as follows:
- My choices about the time, rewards, and location of my future work are not affected by the health or age of myself or my family.
- Periodic but temporary health requirements may affect my choices about the time, rewards, and location of my future work (e.g., occasional medical treatment requiring hospitalization or travel).
- The health and/or age of myself or another family member will significantly affect my choices about the time, rewards, and location of my future work.
- Other

Summary and Reaction:
- **How will health/age factors influence the timing, reward, or location of my future work?**
- **How do I feel about this?**
- **How will I respond to this reality?**

PRIMARY RELATIONSHIPS

How people close to you (spouse, partner, children, housemates) feel about your future work can be an important consideration in what you decide to do. These people are part of the givens of your life. You want to take seriously their expectations about the ways you work. For example, Polly, a corporate vice president, requests that her husband, Sam, a professor, be available when the school nurse calls about their ill child. Sam agrees to make this his responsibility and so arranges for this possibility with his supervisor.

What practical dimensions of work do those close to me want me to consider?
- 40-hour work week with no overtime
- No weekend work
- Limited travel
- Availability for emergency child responsibility
- Other

Summary and Reaction:
- **What practical dimensions of work do those close to me want me to consider?**
- **How do I feel about this?**
- **How will I respond to this reality?**

3

Once you define your path, if you continue to take even small steps, you will eventually be standing on the threshold of your goal.

Carolyn Jabs
"How to Kick a Dream Into Action"[3]

Bust Loose

If you feel like something's got to give, chances are the time is ripe for change. Before her children arrived, Karen worked as a fashion merchandizer in a department store. She loved it. Hours were long, but she didn't care. She was in her element.

When her first child was born, conflict tore her apart. Child care arrangements proved unsatisfactory. On the job she found herself worrying more about her baby than about her customers. She knew it was time for a change. Again and again she felt herself thinking: "I want to stay at home with my baby."

But another reality would not let her go: "I want to earn my share of the family expenses."

What to do? She, her husband, and friends began brainstorming about how she could do what she loved, earn what she needed, and also remain at home with the baby.

"Work weekends and earn comp time," said one.

"How about night work — have you ever considered that?"

"Do you know that you can obtain work-at-home contracts from large corporations? Have you thought about that?"

"What about creating a home-based business?"

The suggestions flew. At first confused, Karen gradually sifted the ideas until two surfaced. "I know I want to work at home now so

I can be available to the baby anytime, but I don't want to work for someone else — I'd like to think about creating my own business."

That conclusion led her to start talking with others who had done the same. Enrolling in a Small Business Administration course, she learned what it would take to establish her own business. "I want to do it," she exclaimed, "and I think I can." She knew she enjoyed sales and marketing, and environmental concerns had long held her interest. When a position as regional manager for a company that markets greeting cards made of recycled paper came to her attention, she grabbed it, knowing that she could control much of her schedule and use her home as her primary office.

 Look over the work you did on the Practical Parameters Inventory in Segment 2. Select the parameter that you most want to change. Create a notebook page or card for this parameter and identify the specific result you want.

Brainstorm changes you could make that would bring this result about. If you need some help, ask a friend or two to join in. Remember, brainstorming means anything goes. Be crazy, wild, think of outlandish things, easy or hard — whatever might bring about the result you want.

Now sift a bit, letting two or three feasible steps surface in your mind. Write these steps on your page or card. Resolve to take these steps as soon as possible. Feel good about making a start.

Repeat this process for other parameters you want to change.

One last thought on changing parameters. If there are certain parameters you'd like to change but can't do anything about right now, create a dream box. In that box place a few of your way-out wishes that, if they came true, would place you closer to your dream job. Like:

"I would love to work in a forest."

"I wish I was earning enough money to put my kids through college."

"I would love to move to Arizona and get rid of my allergies."

"I wish I had the time to write science fiction screenplays."

Every once in a while, look in your dream box. You'll be surprised how your dreams have changed without your doing anything about them. Either your dream will be stronger, in which case you might have more momentum to make the changes you want. Or it will not matter as much anymore, and you can throw the item away with no regrets. Have fun!

4

My own behaviour baffles me.
For I find myself not doing
what I really want to do . . . .

St. Paul
Romans 7:15[4]

Dragons You Must Slay

Are you like St. Paul? You decide to make a change and then find yourself avoiding action?

Well, welcome to the human race. That is what many of us do. It's not that unusual. There are forces within and outside that oppose change.

You tell the boss that you want to switch from full to part-time work so that you'll have more time to take care of your sick husband.

Accustomed to having your full-time services, the boss puts up resistance. That's natural. It can cause you to doubt your decision and look for other alternatives.

More difficult to understand are inner forces that sabotage your best intentions. Ray wanted to direct a peace institute after retiring from the military and was willing to take a substantial pay cut to do so. "But then, I began to have second thoughts. This culture equates people's worth with the amount of money they earn. I know I could live on less and am willing to do that, but all of a sudden I find myself worrying about losing face with my friends who are in high-paying jobs."

Elizabeth O'Connor wrote a book entitled *Our Many Selves* in which she describes the many parts of ourselves that compete for attention.[5] Like unruly people who disrupt meetings, these inner selves cry out to be heard. As Ray did, it is usually important to listen to what each inner self is saying and to figure out what each self really needs. They may cause contradictory feelings and unexpected responses:

> "To my surprise, my husband and children offered to help with chores around the house so I could have more time to explore my options. Now I find myself resisting this offer and feeling afraid."

> "I was discussing with a friend my frustration over the lack of time I have to put into this search. She opened a door by offering to take my child once a week. Now I'm feeling overwhelmed with how best to use the time."

Sometimes conflicting feelings don't surface as ambivalence and confusion, but as self-sabotage: forgetting to make a phone call, getting sick on the day of an interview, feeling like you'd rather stay home and read than go to the class for which you just signed up. Change is scary, and sometimes the price is higher than you anticipated. But life without challenge and risk can kill creativity and dampen your spirit. Your inner self may be feeling not only afraid, but discounted in some way. If you take the time to listen to your feelings and to get some reinforcement from people who care for you, you will find it easier to risk changes in your life.

 Take another look at the practical parameter(s) you want to change (Segment 3). Jot down any feelings you have about the steps you have listed. Put a star by those feelings which might block you in carrying your plan forward.

If there are inner or outer forces blocking your efforts to make specific changes in your parameters, write briefly (or draw) in response to these questions:

- What are these forces? Name them.
- What are their characteristics? Describe them.
- What are they saying to you? Write out their messages.
- What is underneath their message — what do they really want? Describe their needs.

Be quiet for a while and reflect on what you wrote. Perhaps change your activity — go for a brief walk or do something around the house. Then write in response to these questions:

- Is there something else that you can do to give recognition to these forces?
- Is there something else that you can do to prevent them from derailing your intention to change your parameters?

5

The style and character of my work developed from the "givens" of my life. My husband was in the military and I needed a job that was moveable. I developed my gifts as a potter and used potting as a teaching tool in churches, workshops, and conference events.

Conversation with a friend

Two Sides of the Coin

Let's face it. Not all parameters can be changed.

Take Harry for example. "Everyone said that I had it made when I married Natasha. She's got a great job pulling down big money in some hot-shot law firm downtown. But to tell you the truth, it's put a crimp in my wanderlust. We're stuck in Seattle."

OK, Harry's not going anywhere. But he's made peace with that "fixed" portion of his life. "I love Tasha. I want to be with her and I want the best for her. So over time I've taken that old restlessness and channelled it into other pursuits. I've been counseling runaways. You gotta know I can feel where they're coming from."

Segment 1 introduced the idea that fixed parameters, freely chosen, point to another priority that is being supported. Hank and Joy are a two-career couple. "Equality of job opportunity is of central concern in our relationship," says Joy. Hank echoes her thought: "We don't have the kind of marriage where one of us always follows the other. We take turns." "When I was offered a position in Boston," Joy explains, "Hank transferred. Then it was his turn. When his career dictated that we move to Akron, I gritted my teeth and found new work there." For Hank and Joy, equality is a value sufficiently strong to dictate where they will work.

Parameters that seem fixed can also help you decide on certain kinds of work. They give you information about job choice that must be weighed in with other factors. After Louise finished graduate school in human resource development, she was determined to obtain a position using that skill. But at age sixty-five, she was also feeling tired. The jobs she could find in her field were all a long commuting distance away. A workplace close to home was what she wanted. In the end, this was the deciding factor in her acceptance of a job not precisely in her field, but near to home.

Fixed parameters do cut off certain kinds of choice. In so doing, they form a framework for your decisions, point to important choices already made, and provide valuable information about the vocational choices still before you.

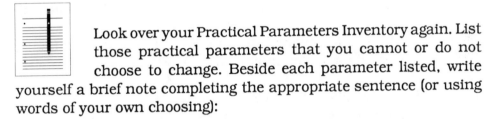 Look over your Practical Parameters Inventory again. List those practical parameters that you cannot or do not choose to change. Beside each parameter listed, write yourself a brief note completing the appropriate sentence (or using words of your own choosing):

- I feel peaceful about this parameter because . . .
- This parameter expresses my commitment to . . .
- This parameter helps me decide about future work because . . .

To enrich what you have done, use your right brain to shine a different light on one or more of the fixed parameters that shape your choices. Think up some metaphors:

- This situation feels like . . .
  - reminds me of . . .
    - is just like . . .

Have fun with this part of the exercise. What light does humor throw on the situation?

GATHERING

Purpose: *To experience support and feedback from others as you deal with changing some practical priorities and valuing others; to take stock of where you and your group are in the "working from the heart" process*

Everyone Bring: *Results of activities from Segments 3 and 5*

Warm-Up (Everyone)   **15 minutes**

Share briefly your feelings related to doing activities of this chapter. You might ask:

- What did I learn about myself?
- Do I generally give too much or not enough attention to practical parameters?

Support and Feedback (Three's)   **20 minutes**

1. Take turns sharing some of the parameters you want to change, the results you want, and steps you have taken or will take (from Segment 3).
2. Ask for further ideas and feedback. Jot down what seems useful.
3. Ask for on-going support or accountability in carrying out your steps.

Encouragement and Affirmation (Four's)   **25 minutes**

1. Look over the work you did in Segment 5 on practical parameters you cannot or choose not to change.
2. Select from this list one practical parameter you want to talk about.
3. Take turns reading aloud your sentence completions and metaphors for that parameter.
4. Listeners affirm reader's choices and clarity.
5. If time, have a free discussion on topics raised.

Take Stock (Everyone)   **25 minutes**

Since you now have met several times together and worked through several chapters alone, this is a good time to take stock of how you are progressing personally and together. Based on what you discover, make changes in the way you are taking part in your group or partnership.

1.   Spend 5 minutes in silence and reflect on:
     a. How do you think you are doing in the "working from the heart" process?
     b. What changes would you like to make?
     c. How do you think the group is (the two of you are) working together?
     d. What changes would you like to make?
2.   Share reflections with the whole group (each other).

Closing (Everyone)   **5 minutes**

7

Letting go of certainties, reframing the central question, spotting the wrong questions, using errors and failure — all these steps are fundamental in seeking the creative solution.

Gail Sheehy
Pathfinders[6]

A Fresh Look

Have you ever flown in a helicopter or a small plane? The experience is both exhilarating and humbling — gazing down on hills, streams, roads, and neighborhoods previously explored on foot.

In a sense, that was the point of this chapter. Occasionally it helps to remove yourself from the niggling details of daily life and gain a little perspective.

From the ground, parameters can seem like mountains too tall to scale, rivers too wide to cross, but from the perspective of your whole life, things look more hopeful. Either you can summon the resources you need to change your situation, or you can recognize that situation for what it is — the product of choices you have made and of which you feel proud.

Stepping back and surveying the contours of your life is not a one-shot deal. Practical parameters shift with the passage of time. When that happens, it helps to use the tools offered here and take stock yet again.

Take another look at the work you did in the activities for Segments 3 and 5. Based on what you learned in the Gathering session, are there any changes you want to make? When you are satisfied with the steps you plan to take, begin or continue to carry them out.

On the Summary Page for this chapter, enter the parameters that shape your choices and indicate any you want to change.

Choose and Explore

Why is it I get my best ideas in the morning while I'm shaving?

Albert Einstein
quoted by Rollo May
The Courage to Create[1]

The Heart of the Matter: Choosing a Focus

It's time to choose a vocational focus. "But, but, but," you may sputter, "I'm not ready for this." Yes, that may be true, but the very act of choosing sets things in motion. Crazy as it may seem, if you make a choice, jump in, and start to explore, sparks will fly and things will happen. Momentum will build, insights will come, and you may find that your first choice yields genuine fruit — or perhaps leads to something more productive to explore.

So even if you don't think you're ready, plunge into this chapter and complete the activities that address the key question:

**What vocational focus do I want to choose
and how will I explore it?**

Just off the top of your head, what is your first response to the question, "What vocational focus do you want to explore?" Write down your immediate, gut-level response in your notebook or on a card.

Be as free as possible, even if the idea seems impractical or silly. If you always wanted to be an artist, write that down. Do you have talents you rarely use and want to pursue? Would you like to apply proven skills to a new field? Maybe you'd like more room for creativity and originality in your present job. For now, let reality go out the window. Don't ponder too long; go with your instinctive feeling. Name one field or subject you'd love to investigate. Do as Brenda Ueland urges: "Be careless, reckless! Be a lion, be a pirate! . . . disconnect all shackles, weights, obligations, all duties."[2]

You may have to sneak up on yourself to answer this question. Try redirecting your energy for a few minutes. Take a walk, straighten up something around the house, make a cup of tea, go to the bathroom. Yes, we all know it, great insights occur often in the bathroom!

Then ask again: What vocational focus do I want to explore? Jot down or draw whatever comes.

When you've chosen a focus, post it some place where you'll run into it — on a mirror, on the fridge, on a counter. Let it percolate for a day. Wear it like a new coat. See how it feels.

2

Creative people make connections. Making connections is bringing together seemingly unrelated ideas, objects, or events in a way that leads to a new conception.

"Creativity: The Human Resource"
a pamphlet by Frank Barron[3]

A Second Look

Remember as a kid when you first looked through a kaleidoscope? You saw a picture; then, with a slight turn, the pieces formed a new pattern of shapes and colors, rewarding you with another delightful visual feast.

Sometimes a small change of vantage point can give you another way to see the components of your life. You take a second look, and a different pattern emerges, giving you fresh insight and direction. Sometimes this happens in a flash, as the activity for Segment 1 suggested. But new insight and direction may also emerge as a result of a more reflective look at your life.

At forty-five, Joyce was disheartened with her work as a budget analyst for a large government agency. Finally, one day she quit.

> Everyone was flabbergasted because I was so good at my job. But I was sick of it for several reasons. I was tired of being a boss — it really is lonely at the top. That's not just a cliché. I longed for real friendships on the job, not simply "good working relationships." Also, work with figures can get old. Sure, I was powerful — allocating big sums to various projects. But something was missing."

In her search for the missing pieces, Joyce identified her gifts, but nothing new turned up, just her strong skills in business and management which had always been there. She reflected further:

> I longed for beauty — flowers, art, music — the parts of life usually associated with re-creation and creativity. The trouble was that I didn't have talent in those fields. Yet my love for them seemed to be increasing. I kept wondering what this was telling me. Then one day I put my love of the arts together with my management skills, and suddenly it dawned on me — maybe I could explore arts management.

Continuing her progression of thought, she added:

> I began to wonder if I could find a way to work more *with* people and not always above or below them. And then I thought that if I worked in a fledgling operation, I might have more of that feeling of being creative and working on a team. These ideas sparked me, and I began to think of people I could talk with about this.

Give yourself some time today to take a reflective look at your life. Think about all the work you have done so far with this book and allow it to inform your choice of which vocational focus to explore. Spread out your Summary Pages, journal entries, cards, and any other materials you have gathered thus far in your search. In addition, you might want to set out some favorite possessions that represent something of value to you: a treasured book, or stone, or photograph. If you remember a persistent dream or an important conversation that seems illuminating, write down its essence and place that before you as well.

Become quiet and then allow yourself to focus on all these reminders of who you are and what you most want to do with your life. Let these general questions guide your initial reflection. Write down what occurs to you.

- What type of commitment is illustrated by the things I've chosen as important to me?
- As I contemplate future work possibilities, what in this material makes a strong impression on me?
- Does any part of this material cause an emotional response — tearful, joyful, angry, frustrated, wistful?
- Where in this material does the most energy and excitement exist for me?

Then address these more specific questions either in writing or by drawing something:

- Do I prefer working with **people, data,** or **things** (or some combination of these)?
- With what **subject** or **issue** would I like to be involved?
- What **skills** do I especially want to use in work?

Answer these questions with as much clarity as you now have. When you are ready, ask yourself again, **"What vocational focus do I want to explore?"** In your notebook or on a card write what thoughts occur to you. This may add to or modify what you wrote in Segment 1.

If more than one possibility occurs to you, then select one to explore for now. The information-gathering skills you use to investigate this possibility can be used later to explore others.

3

I'm a great believer in libraries — and in librarians, bless them. You can go to the library in any moderate-sized town, college, or university and find out almost anything you need to know, from the regulations of the American Kennel Club to the Gross National Product of Paraguay.

Barbara Sher with Annie Gottlieb
Wishcraft[4]

Sleuth Your Way to Clarity

You've chosen your area to explore, and you may be asking questions such as:

"Could I possibly turn my love of photography into a business?"

"My heart reaches out to the underdog. How can I find work with an oppressed group that will earn me enough money to provide for my family?"

"Accounting skills got me my job in this huge company. I wonder whether I could find another position in the organization that uses my people skills?"

Now is the time to begin finding out the answers to such questions. All vocational exploration methods boil down to three familiar activities you engage in every day of your life: **talk, read,** and **experience.** Which you do and in what combination depends on the kind of person you are.

When Ken wondered if he could convert his photography hobby into a business, he decided to talk with people who make their living from photography. When Betty heard about Ken's intention, she protested, "I hate talking to people I don't know, and especially about a topic I'm not sure of. But give me something to read and I'm in seventh heaven." Emily said, "I learn best through experience. I can't stand having people explain things to me — in person or on paper. Put me in a situation and let me start doing something. I'll learn once I'm involved."

It's probably good to use all three methods of exploration in some sort of combination. But feel free to place the emphasis on what is most motivating to you. Think of yourself as Sherlock Holmes collecting fragments, clues, bits and pieces of information that slowly fit together into a meaningful whole.

TALK

Once you zero in on something you're interested in and start talking about it, it's surprising how soon and how frequently you run into people who know something about the subject. When Henry decided he wanted to investigate the field of city management, he discovered that a friend of a friend knew the manager of a neighboring town and was willing to arrange for him to meet with her.

In our seminars, we often set up what we call a "resource merry-go-round." On notebook sheets, people describe the kind of help they need. Then, taking turns, they place these sheets on a chair in the center of the circle, briefly describe their situation, and invite people to sign if they have information to offer. People have asked, "Who knows something about marketing a book . . . doing theater with disadvantaged kids . . . learning landscape design . . . boosting office morale?"

Almost always someone in the room has a clue. We are surrounded by people who know things we need to know or who can help us find someone who does.

READ

Let your intuition guide you here. Read what you want. And read with two perspectives in mind. You are learning the wisdom of another — that is true. But more important is "reflective reading," that is, reading to get more in touch with your own uniqueness. In school, you were probably taught to master the major points of what an author covered, remember them, and be ready to regurgitate them at exam time. With reflective reading, the important thing is what resonates with you: one particular point, a phrase, a reference to another work, a brief quotation, an impression.

Go to the library, browse in bookstores, write to organizations for literature, and track down some reading material that will help you answer your vocational questions. The more you look, the more you'll find.

Pam, who was interested in working with the handicapped, at first confined herself to reading books on the subject. In exploring further, she found the National Information Center for Handicapped Children and Youth and requested their brochure, "Investigating Careers in Service to People with Special Needs." Many more associations than you imagine are devoted to providing information and resources on specific vocational fields, and on specialties within those fields. Pam wanted to incorporate sports into her work with the handicapped, so she obtained and read material from such organizations as Ski for Light, Inc., devoted to teaching visually impaired people to ski. What she found was a goldmine of information available for the price of a postcard.

When you read material related to the subject you are investigating, use questions like these to guide your reflections:

- What points resonate with me?
- What do they tell me about my particular "work from the heart"?
- What further lines of inquiry do they suggest?

EXPERIENCE

Think of experience as falling into two categories: personal exposure and training.

Personal exposure means placing yourself in a work setting where you meet practitioners or join in the actual work. There are a whole range of activities that fall into this category.

For example, if you want an immediate feel of a particular field, **tag along** for a day or two with someone working in that field. Or **volunteer** for a short time and try your hand at actually doing some of the work yourself. Or **apply for an internship position.** (This usually requires a firm time commitment on your part in exchange for on-the-job training.) You may also want to try **temporary work,**

part-time work, or **vacation work** (assisting on an archaelogical dig, for example) with a person or organization working in a field that interests you.

Jennifer, an organic farming student, was not sure about the kind of farm on which she wanted to work. She decided to visit a series of farms, working for three weeks at each one in return for room and board. On the third farm, she met a grower who was starting an agricultural experiment in Mexico. Sensing her enthusiasm, the grower asked Jennifer if she wanted to help in that project. Not only did Jennifer find paid work, but she also realized how much agriculture in the developing nations interested her.

Another way to get personal experience is to **affiliate** with a professional or vocational organization active in your field. This will give you a different kind of opportunity to associate with people working in your area of interest. By serving with them on committees and task forces, you can try your hand at doing the kind of work you think you may want to do in the future. You will also learn of job opportunities and conferences in your field.

As you gain some hands-on experience, continually ask yourself,

- How do I like working in this field?
- Do I like the kinds of people who are doing the kind of work I am investigating?
- Do I like the projects they undertake?

The second category of experience is training that will teach you more about your area of interest and your potential involvement in it.

It is surprising how often people think of obtaining a graduate degree in order to see what kind of work they want to do. We strongly advise against this as a first move. Graduate work has its place, but our suggestion is to do some investigation before jumping into such a large commitment of time and money. Here are some ways to test the waters:

- **Workshops and conferences** involve a minimum investment of time, energy, and money, and are usually packed with useful information and activities. They teach skills, help participants network with each other, and present additional resource material.
- **Short continuing education courses** introduce you to more formal education in the field you are investigating. An initial taste may help you decide whether you want more education or not. Find out if the material of the course energizes you or puts you to sleep.

If after careful investigation, a full academic or vocational program seems to be the next step, be sure to choose the program wisely. Ask if it will prepare you to realize your working goal. Check the reputation of the school, the department, and the faculty.

Finding the best training to fit your particular needs is worth the time it takes to do it. A good training decision can take you far along your vocational path. A poor one can waste time and money and cause discouragement. More thoughts on training are included in Appendix 1.

However you investigate your area of focus — through talking, reading, experience, or a combination of the three — it's important to frame good questions. These evolve as you gain new information. You will want to ask such questions as:

- What are the various kinds of positions open in the field?
- What are the requirements to qualify for these positions?
- What kinds of activities are carried out by people in these positions?
- Who is involved in the kind of thing I want to investigate?
- Where can I find reading material that is pertinent?

Create a notebook page or card with the heading **Questions**. List all the questions you can think of that you need to have answered in order to know whether this is what you want to do.

Create three additional pages or cards with the headings **Talk, Read,** and **Experience.** Brainstorm as many ideas as possible about people to talk with, reading to consider, and experiences to try. Write them down on the appropriate pages or cards.

This is a beginning. Update and modify your lists as you think of new questions and gather new information.

. . . when you go out interviewing for information, both of you will be talking to each other about a mutual Enthusiasm — not just passing the time of day, talking about the weather.

Richard Nelson Bolles
The Three Boxes of Life and How to Get Out of Them[5]

Interviewing for Information

At some point in your investigation you will want to talk with people in depth. "Interviewing for Information" (see Appendix 2) is an invaluable skill that you can use not only in your vocational search, but also to explore any new subject. In terms of your vocational search, interviewing for information means talking with people who are doing the kind of work you are exploring — about anything you want to know concerning that area.

You can have a lot of fun with this technique. First choose people you know — colleagues or friends who are easy to talk to and with whom you feel comfortable. Gradually you will feel confident about reaching beyond the familiar to people you don't know who are engaged in the field you are exploring. Sure, you may feel nervous. That's natural for most people. But remember: You'll be talking about things that fascinate you.

What if you don't hit it off with someone? Don't worry about it. You're searching for the people and ways of working that do click with you. Life is too short to be involved with people you don't like or who don't appreciate your interest in their line of work.

So be brave and creative in selecting people to interview: co-workers who love what they're doing; students attending the training program you're considering; writers who have produced material in your field of interest. It only takes a phone call and a request. Nine out of ten people you ask will be delighted to spend an hour being an expert in their speciality or a consultant in your situation.

Interviewing for information can be done formally by appointment or casually over coffee with a colleague. In either case, be prepared and conscious of what you want to receive from the interview.

Maggie, for example, wondered whether she really wanted work in the field of economic justice. She decided to interview George, the director of a local justice center. To make the best use of their time together, Maggie did some homework. Reading the center literature gave her an overview of its mission. Listing her questions in writing helped her focus on what she wanted to learn. This included information on the kinds of jobs available in the field, how much money she could earn in what type of justice work, and tips on next steps she could take to pursue her interest.

You can always learn something from an interview — another person to contact, an article to read, a place to visit. When done well, interviewing for information can yield valuable information, as well as create a network of people who know and care about your progress in finding work.

But there are pitfalls. An interview with someone who is well established in your field of interest can make you feel discouraged about the long road ahead. You might feel disappointed or frustrated if the interview did not seem to go well. Interviewing for information takes practice. Appendix 2 contains a full description of how to prepare, conduct, and debrief yourself after such an interview.

Read "Interviewing for Information" in Appendix 2 of this book.

Review the list you prepared in Segment 3 of people you want to talk with. Select one with whom to begin an interview.

Write a brief description of this interviewee — their position, their area of experience or knowledge, and why you want to interview them.

Write a brief self-description, as suggested in #4 under the section Preparation, in "Interviewing for Information."

Prepare several questions that you would like your interviewee to answer for you. Be sure to include some questions dealing with the person's objective knowledge of the field, and some questions asking for help and advice related to your own situation.

Organize, don't agonize.

5

Motto of Tish Sommers, founder, Older Women's League (OWL)[6]

Take Tish Sommer's Advice

So far the work of this chapter has encouraged you to think of ways you could investigate your area of vocational focus. Now is the time to organize for action — to plan specific steps you will take within a given time frame. This will be your Vocational Exploration Plan. It will include the vocational focus you intend to explore, plus several steps you can take now to get moving.

Most people, once they get started, make a series of Vocational Exploration Plans, either on paper or in their minds, each one building on the last as their knowledge of their field expands.

Take Henry: Discouraged with his job and confused about his direction, Henry knew only that he wanted to explore the field of city management. You may recall from Segment 3 that a friend of a friend knew the manager of a neighboring city and was willing to put Henry in contact with her. While setting up the appointment, the manager told Henry about the International Association of City Managers, which Henry visited the next day. While waiting for the manager to see him he read some of the Association's newsletters. From the interview itself, Henry learned about training requirements and job opportunities in the field.

Finding that many of these positions required a Master's degree, which he did not have and did not currently wish to obtain, Henry's line of questioning narrowed. He began asking informed people whether it was possible to obtain a manager's job without a graduate degree if the town were small enough and could not afford someone with a Master's degree. The answer was yes. So Henry decided to visit Vermont, a state full of small towns, to look into town manager position listings for which he could qualify.

Once he focused in and began telling others what he was looking for, people began calling him. His cousin told him about a position in Virginia; an old work buddy from Maine described an opening he knew about. Things began to happen. As Henry worked hard to explore various opportunities, other people came up with additional leads. His mood changed. He no longer felt discouraged. "Now I have confidence that there's a job out there that's right for me. But it's going to take work, patience, and perseverance to find it."

Henry's story is still unfolding. A month ago he was in a fog about the future. Now he has direction and is on his way. Each step led to another. His evolving Vocational Exploration Plans, which he thought about in his head, looked like this in writing:

Vocational Exploration Plan 1

Area to explore: city management
Steps: 1. talk with city manager — tomorrow
2. read material in her office — tomorrow

Vocational Exploration Plan 2

Area to explore: city management
Steps: 1. talk with city management association — Dec. 1
2. read material in that office — Dec. 1

Vocational Exploration Plan 3

Area to explore: small town management
Steps: 1. go to Vermont — Dec. 10
2. talk with as many people as I can about government and ask how to break into small-town management — Dec. 10-14

Well, you get the idea. Now it's your turn.

On a notebook page or card, create a blank Vocational Exploration Plan, like the one shown on the next page.

Enter the vocational focus you have chosen on the form you have created. In Segment 3, you started a running list of questions plus three resource lists (people to talk to, reading, and experience) of ways to find answers. Review these resource lists and circle several items that seem most do-able now. That will get the ball rolling. Enter these as steps on your Vocational Exploration Plan form and put a date next to each. Label this your Vocational Exploration Plan 1.

<u>Vocational Exploration Plan</u>

Focus to explore: _____

_____

Steps:

	Action	Date
1.	_____	_____
2.	_____	_____
3.	_____	_____

As you think through your Vocational Exploration Plan, you may, like Henry, be aware that you need a particular kind of help but don't have any resources. Create a "Help Wanted" notebook page or card listing specific kinds of help you need. Resolve to talk with two people in the next two days about what you need.

GATHERING

6

Purpose: *To practice interviewing for information; to describe your Vocational Exploration Plan 1 and to obtain help on it*
Everyone Bring:
Interviewee description from Segment 4
Self-description from Segment 4
Interview questions from Segment 4
Vocational Exploration Plan 1 from Segment 5
Help Wanted list from Segment 5

Warm-Up (Everyone)   **10 minutes**

Briefly check with each other on how it felt to choose a vocational focus. Everyone share a word or two.

Role Play Interview (Two's or Three's)   **60 minutes**

This activity is designed for pairs, but if you are meeting with a group, you might like to experiment with a threesome — an interviewer, an interviewee, and an observer to give feedback in the debriefing period. During this activity, you will have a chance to introduce yourself and to ask questions in a simulated interview using role-play techniques. The content of the role play should be based on the real-life situation of the interviewer and the "created on the spot" responses of the person being interviewed for information. Both people will have a chance to play both roles. (If an observer is used, you will need to structure the time differently so the third person also has the opportunity to role play with someone.)

Note: Obviously, the person being interviewed will have to make up answers to the questions being asked. Keep in mind that it is not the content of the information that is important here, but the experience of what it is like to interview someone.

1. **Preparation** (5 minutes):
    Interviewer gives partner written description of person they are to play. As interviewee reads the description and prepares for the role play, the interviewer looks over his or her self-description and questions and prioritizes them.
2. **Interview** (20 minutes):
    Interviewer asks questions about the particular field of interest and requests specific suggestions about his or her personal situation.
3. **Debriefing** (5 minutes):
    Exchange a brief critique on how the interviewer did and what could be improved.
4. **Repeat** the process, reversing roles (30 minutes).

Encouragement and Help (Everyone)   15 minutes

1. Share your Vocational Exploration Plan.
2. Name the help you need. If you are gathering with a group, put your "Help Wanted" list in the center of the circle.
3. Those who have ideas about how to help should sign their names and phone numbers on the sheet. (If you are doing this exercise with a partner, exchange your lists and brainstorm possible resources.)
4. After everyone has shared, send each other off with words of encouragement.

Closing (Everyone)   5 minutes

7

A willingness to risk is the master quality for pathfinding. Because it is the linchpin, I have taken it up first, despite the fact that it is the most difficult quality to cultivate and requires the greatest strength.

. . . It would be convenient if there were bromides for instant strength, and splendid if they could be reduced to self-help formulas. Unfortunately, strength is built layer by layer.

Gail Sheehy
Pathfinders[7]

Off You Go

You've chosen a focus to explore, learned ways to investigate it, selected specific steps to begin, received help from others, and practiced interviewing.

Now is the time to begin exploring your vocational focus. Feeling excited or a bit nervous? Probably a bit of both.

Defining what constitutes meaningful work is like shopping for clothes or records or books. Some people love the open-ended search. Others don't. Either way, the name of the game is to try things on — clothing, musical tastes, literary genres. A good shopper will tell you to try on what immediately appeals, but also to experiment. That's the way to get to know yourself better. "Oh no! This is too bright on me." "Hey, I didn't know I liked jazz!" "What an extraordinary poet; I'd never heard of him." "This color makes the kind of statement I feel good about wearing!"

For some, an invitation to shop is a chance to relax and have fun. It's a no-risk proposition — a chance for uninhibited expression and trying new things. For others, the prospect is slightly more appealing than a ten-year jail sentence. For these folks, so much to choose from and no real way to make a choice is a curse.

Know who you are. If vocational exploration comes easy, celebrate that fact and enjoy the experience. If it comes hard, know that the reward is sweet and solid when it comes.

In this chapter you've been challenged to choose an occupational field to explore. No one is saying that this is what you will end up doing for the rest of your life. In choosing a focus to investigate — any focus — you are taking a valuable step. You are learning how to investigate a field of interest and thereby gaining information. Your Vocational Exploration Plan is an unfolding, ever-evolving document. Completion of one step will give birth to ten new ideas on how to proceed. Let the energy you feel as you finish one step motivate you to articulate and complete next steps.

As you talk with friends and professionals, read relevant writings, and taste experientially that which you think you might want to do, not only will your plan evolve, but the very way you think about your future work may grow or shift. Don't resist this process. Embrace it. It means you are getting closer.

One last tip: Don't run out of steps to take. Always have a few in your hip pocket. Why? If one strategy doesn't pan out the way you'd hoped, having another in mind can help you recoup more easily. It's like the wise writer who always has another copy of her manuscript addressed and ready to send to the next publisher if, as will happen, the mail brings a rejection notice. It's just a fact of life that some steps lead nowhere. Expect it. When it happens, go back to the fork in the road and take another route.

If you have not done so, contact those who offered help during the Gathering session to obtain their ideas. Incorporate into your Vocational Exploration Plan any modifications that occur to you as a result of the Gathering session or the input of people in your group.

Enter your Plan on the Summary Page for this chapter.

Congratulate yourself on the progress you've made. Begin to carry out your plan.

Call in Reinforcements

Very few people ever make it alone. We all need someone to lead the way, to show us the ropes, to tell us the norms, to encourage, support, and make it a little easier for us. Who are these people who will do that and where do we find them? They have been called benefactors, godfathers, patrons, rabbis.

Natasha Josefowitz
Paths to Power[1]

People Power

"Without him I could not be doing what I'm doing."[2] These words were spoken by a graduate at the death of Father Gilbert Hartke, founder of the Speech and Drama Department, The Catholic University of America. Known for taking students under his wing throughout their university training and well afterward, Father Hartke supported them not only vocationally but personally. He taught, coached, and directed; he probed, prodded, and cheered. With his loving attention, his students were encouraged to do their best.

Other people can make a huge difference in helping you move where you want to go. So far, you have been encouraged to seek out people for information and advice. Now it's time to give attention to the ongoing support you need from people who believe in your potential.

At Christmas, a card came with this inscription:

> . . . the best and most beautiful
> things in the world
> cannot
> be seen nor even touched,
> but just
> felt in the heart.[3]

These words were composed by Helen Keller, the blind, deaf, and mute woman whose unrelenting girlhood temper tantrums had been the despair of her friends and family. What brought her to the place where she could write such tender thoughts?

A crucial factor was the loving, careful instruction given by Helen's teacher, Annie Sullivan, herself handicapped with partial blindness but endowed with a belief in the possibilities that lay within the seemingly hopeless case that was her charge.

Helen's words are particularly touching because they capture the essence of "working from the heart." People who believe in you — the Annie Sullivans, the Gilbert Hartkes, Scout leaders, coaches, teachers, parents, grandparents — encourage and energize you to do work that draws on your best self: work that is first and foremost felt in the heart. You, in turn, become the Annie Sullivan or the Gilbert Hartke to others, believing in their potential, and helping them to make their way.

In the preface to one of her books, *In Search of Our Mothers' Gardens*, Alice Walker puts it beautifully:

> In my development as a human being and as a writer I have been, it seems to me extremely blessed, even while complaining. Wherever I have knocked, a door has opened. Wherever I have wandered, a path has appeared. I have been helped, supported, encouraged, and nurtured by people of all races, creeds, colors, and dreams; and I have, to the best of my ability, returned help, support, encouragement, and nurture. This receiving, returning, or passing on has been one of the most amazing, joyous and continuous experiences of my life.[4]

You too are part of this helping chain. Remember the people who have nurtured you, draw again on their strength, but also reach out now to people who can help you develop further. You may have already started to do this through the interviews planned in Chapter 4. The support of these people will enable you, in turn, to pass on to others the encouragement they offer you.

Chapter 1 included Joseph Campbell's wonderful advice for anyone seeking their life's work: "Follow your bliss." In another part of the same interview, Campbell was asked, "Do you ever have this sense when you are following your bliss . . . of being helped by hidden hands?" Campbell replied:

All the time. It is miraculous. I even have a superstition that has grown on me as the result of invisible hands coming all the time — namely, that if you do follow your bliss you put yourself on a kind of track that has been there all the while, waiting for you, and the life that you ought to be living is the one you are living. When you can see that, you begin to meet people who are in the field of your bliss, and they open doors to you. I say, follow your bliss and don't be afraid, and doors will open where you didn't know they were going to be.[5]

Yes, doors will open. But you must do your share of knocking. A crucial part of that process is to determine who can give you the kind of help you need. Thus, the key question for this chapter:

**Who will be my companions
in my quest for meaningful work?**

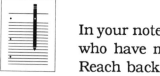 In your notebook or on a card, begin a list of the helpers who have made you what you are. Look around you. Reach back in time. Enjoy remembering who they are. Draw again on the energy they have given you as you record their names.

Create a similar list of the people who you have reached out to help along the way. Remembering the help, support, and encouragement that you have given to others will make it easier for you to ask for the help you need now.

Become conscious of the role of helping people in the lives of people you know or hear about. Remember Geraldine Ferraro naming Tip O'Neill as her mentor? Or Florence Griffith-Joyner attributing her Olympic success to the encouragement of her husband? Keep a lookout for examples like this. They'll encourage you to ask for help when you need it.

2

Will Marion Cook was my mentor. He was a composer and an orchestra man. He had what they call a sweet syncopation orchestra that played sweet jazz, ragtime. They called him Daddy Cook. He was so cantankerous, he wouldn't let you change any note on his music.

Eva Jessye
I Dream a World[6]

Wishing Makes It Possible

To be near her three-year-old daughter, Carol moved her public relations business into her home. The first year was great, but gradually the spark left her work. Finally, she admitted, "I'm lonely. I miss having colleagues to bounce things around with."

"I'd love to start my own business," said Bruce, "but I need to get some advice about the technical details."

Carol wanted colleagues. Bruce wanted an advisor. Both identified helping roles they wished others could play in their vocational lives. They did not know who could fill these roles, only that they wished someone could.

The following People and Vocation Inventory may stimulate your thinking and help you differentiate the kinds of help you need from other people. Remember: No one person can provide everything you'd like at any one time.

As you read each description in the People and Vocation Inventory, decide which are "relevant" and "irrelevant" for you at this point in your quest. If the kind of person described in the inventory could be helpful to you right now, check "relevant." If not, check "irrelevant." Don't worry about being right or thorough; and don't think through the implications of your choices. Just be spontaneous. If you wish you had such a person in your life right now, the inventory description is "relevant." If the description doesn't ring a bell for you now, it's "irrelevant."

PEOPLE AND VOCATION INVENTORY

COLLEAGUE: Someone to work with, or an associate in a similar profession.

Wish:

"I work all alone; I need colleagues."

"I'd like someone to have lunch with who knows my business and with whom I could unwind — brainstorm solutions."

Possibility:

Nan and Terry both work in the field of alternative health care. Nan is a nurse-healer; Terry is a massage therapist. Each has an independent operation, but they look to one another for support and information on shared issues: how to deal with problem clients, what companies to use for advertising, where to locate their offices.

_____ Relevant   _____ Irrelevant

MENTOR: Someone to believe in you who can, over time, help you move forward through guidance and coaching.

Wish:

"I've always wanted someone to take an interest in my progress and to lend a helping hand as I struggle to put things in perspective."

"I need a person who is more than a friend and more than a boss, someone who has contacts, influence, and faith in my abilities."

Possibility:

A writer in the beginning stages of her career, Jane asked her friend, a published author, to read her work. Feeling it had merit, the author took time to encourage her, send her notices of writing seminars, and answer questions as they arose.

_____ Relevant   _____ Irrelevant

SUPERVISOR: Someone to oversee your work and guarantee its quality by the strength of his or her reputation and expertise.

Wish:

"I need someone to supervise my counseling work so I can be certified."

"I'm trying to prepare food in my restaurant according to the theory advanced by a particular nutritionist. I'd love to meet with her once a week for a while until I'm sure I'm doing things right."

Possibility:

Karin, trained in art history, volunteered to write the catalog for a museum art exhibit. She asked the curator to supervise her work. Later, when applying for a paid position in art history, her supervisor's description and recommendation of her work opened the door to paid employment.

_____ Relevant   _____ Irrelevant

ADVISOR: Source of information and counsel in a non-regular and on an informal basis.

Wish:

"I wish I knew someone who could tell me what professional organization I should join."

"I need a resource person to tell me where I can find job listings."

"Do I have to join the union to break into the field? I'd love to talk to someone who really knows this stuff."

Possibility:

Recall Henry (mentioned in Chapter 4), who was pursuing a career in city management. Speaking with Ron, an officer in the professional association, he asked, "Which is my best next step, graduate school or an entry-level position?" Ron replied, "It generally depends on the size of the town or city. Large places want a Master's degree. Smaller towns are willing to consider someone without one, but they pay less."

_____ Relevant   _____ Irrelevant

COLLABORATOR: A person with whom you want to produce something; this can involve anything from a legal working partnership to an occasional productive association.

Wish:

"I feel most productive when working as part of a team."

"My skills are specific but would be more marketable when offered in concert with others."

Possibility:

A talented young New York architect, Pierre wanted to start his own firm. The problem? "I can design houses," he said, "but can't find people who need houses designed. What I'm looking for is someone good at architectural marketing with whom I can join forces."

Pierre thought of two possibilities for collaboration: He could talk with his friend Rosa, who is strong in marketing, about going into business together. Or he could contact his friend Ted's public relations and marketing firm to generate clients with whom he would then work alone.

_____ **Relevant**   _____ **Irrelevant**

PATRON SAINT: Someone to identify with who inspires you.

Wish:

"This is an age without heroes; I want to feel good about someone who has walked this same difficult road before me."

"I need inspiration."

Possibility:

"Dr. Martin Luther King, Jr. has been my life-long inspiration," says Al. "Everything he has written, I have read. When I'm feeling discouraged, I return to Dr. King's quotes, and they give me strength. His struggles motivate my sense of mission."

_____ **Relevant**   _____ **Irrelevant**

FRIEND: A person close to you in whom you can confide your vocational hopes and dreams, failures and successes.

Wish:

"I feel like letting off steam — I'm so confused. I just wish I had somebody to talk with."

"I got a wild idea last night — I think I want to change my career from retail sales to elementary teaching. I need to toss that idea around with someone I trust."

Possibility:

Just before Jill drove off to interview for a job she really wanted, the phone rang. It was Greg. "I'll be thinking of you as you go through the interview. I know you'll do a great job. Be sure to call me as soon as possible after you finish. I'm dying to hear what happened." This was not the first time this had occurred. Greg, of all her friends, had supported Jill through the stops and starts of her vocational meanderings. He really was interested. Jill felt it and was grateful.

_____ **Relevant**   _____ **Irrelevant**

TEACHER: Someone to impart knowledge or offer training in skills you need; this can involve anything from Annie Sullivan's intense relationship with Helen Keller to getting tips from an office mate over a cup of coffee.

Wish:

"My new computer baffles me. I don't have time for a whole course. I wish someone would sit down with me for a couple of hours and get me started."

"People have told me for years that my writing is awful. But I want to learn to write anyway. I need a teacher that will be really patient with me."

Possibility:

After Meg attended a seminar on meeting facilitation, she was eager to share her knowledge. Rhea and Jan invited her over for the evening to talk about her new interest. This gave Meg a chance to solidify her new skills and Rhea and Jan some new information to upgrade theirs.

_____ Relevant   _____ Irrelevant

PATRON: Someone to value your work, support it or become a consumer of it, and in so doing, pass the word about it to others or enable it to be continued.

Wish:

"I love creating my paintings. What I need are people to buy them and expose them to others."

Possibility:

Patroning frequently occurs in the arts. For example, Ken, a hairdresser, agreed to display Pat's watercolors in his shop. But patroning occurs outside of the arts as well. When Nate wanted to enter a monastery, he lacked the resources to make the transition. His friend Abigail gave him two hundred dollars to support his new venture. Nate had found a patron.

_____ Relevant   _____ Irrelevant

SPIRITUAL GUIDE: Someone to support your spiritual quest and care how that is expressed in work; this can involve anything from the friend wise in spiritual ways to clergy or others specially trained to offer spiritual companionship to others.

Wish:

"I'm excited by my faith, but religion stops at the church doors. It doesn't relate to my work at all."

"I have an active spiritual life, though nonreligious. Classes are not enough. I need a coach."

"I feel spiritually dead. I wish I could find someone to talk to about it."

Possibility:

In conversation with a neighbor, Bill learned that there was a spiritual formation center in his city that trained people to offer spiritual guidance. He contacted the center and got the names of several people who were available to offer the companionship he was looking for.

   _____ **Relevant**   _____ **Irrelevant**

OTHER: If necessary, add one or more roles not on this list which you think would be helpful to you.

Wish:

Possibility:

List in your notebook or on cards the "helper" roles you decided were relevant. This list will likely change and evolve as you progress in your search.

3

One plus a friend plus a friend
plus a friend don't say that makes four
the whole is greater than the sum of its parts
small numbers mean friendship
large ones revolution.

Dorothee Sölle
"For My Young Comrades"[7]

It's Open Season on Support: Go Hunting

"You've asked me to change the baby's diapers, listen to how your interview went — plus fix dinner while you write a thank you note. That's too much!" Jack was frustrated and angry. His wife's vocational search was getting on his nerves. It seemed that Sally not only wanted him to shoulder more of the housework and childcare, but also expected him to be available to her for advice and ideas on her quest.

"But I need your help," protested Sally. She did need Jack's help — but was it fair to ask him for *all* the assistance she required? "I'm doing my best to take care of all the household and childcare responsibilities," he said. "Is it too much to ask that you look to your friends for vocational counseling?"

Of course not. Though upset by Jack's confrontation, Sally realized he had a point and began to think about what she needed to move forward. "Wait a minute," she thought. "If I'm going to figure out what kind of help would move me along further, I've got to take stock of where I am."

So Sally asked her friend Betty if she could come over to talk and review her situation. When Betty heard that Sally was looking for personnel work in the company where she now held a position as bookkeeper, she encouraged Sally to contact someone in the personnel department for more information and counsel.

When Sally did this, she was advised to consider additional training before applying for a personnel job. Sally researched her options for further training and found an instructor at the local community college from whom she could take courses in the field of personnel. No longer so dependent on Jack for support in her vocational quest, she felt more grateful to him for shouldering the household responsibilities. He, in turn, found himself more willing to listen to her progress and offer useful feedback.

In the course of searching for the kind of work she wanted, Sally learned a lot about identifying and getting the assistance she needed.

"Yes, I was expecting too much of Jack. Also, I was embarrassed to ask for help from others. But I've learned that as I'm clear about what I need, people are usually more than willing to help."

 Review your list of the types of helpers who would be most relevant to you in your search for "work from the heart" (from Segment 2). For each helping role, create a notebook page or card like this:

People Help

I need a _____
        (teacher, mentor, etc.)

The help I need from this person is _____

_____

People who might fill this role are: _____

                                    _____

                                    _____

As you think about the assistance you need, be as specific as possible. What do you want from the persons who could help you?

Let some of these "people help" ideas percolate a while before acting on them. We'll return to them in Segment 5.

If we can travel with a band of inner companions, what tests can prove too demanding? . . . We need them to share with us the wisdom of the obvious . . . . this wisdom must be absorbed into us by opening our interior lives — an intimacy of the spirit.

Colman McCarthy
Inner Companions[8]

Support from the Inside

If you're in a spot where you need help from others and feel particularly unable to identify people to contact, or if you want to enrich the support you have, consider the multitude of possibilities that open up when you consider those who can be your *inner* companions. These can be friends, ancestors, famous people — those you know personally or only indirectly. Inner companions are loaded with gifts to help you in your quest. They have wisdom to share.

"My Grandmother Hall's words to me, 'I will bless you to be a blessing' are a continuing motto in my life," says Chris. "Although she died 10 years ago, whenever I think about her I still receive something special." Grandmother Hall resides within Chris as an ever-available presence. She is the kind of "inner companion" Colman McCarthy writes about.

Art was feeling particularly stuck and needed help from someone who knew what that was like. "I just feel bogged down in this search," he explained. "I have a whole list of things to do and don't want to attend to any of them." Art found himself thinking of his former neighbor Fred, now living in distant Thailand. Fred had also had a hard time finding work and was now self-employed as an industrial engineer. Knowing that Fred had weathered the hard times made Art think he could, too.

Simply thinking about a person like Grandmother Hall or Fred can lift your spirits. But you can take this a step further. Enter into an imaginary conversation with that person. In this way more wisdom, guidance, or inspiration can come. One way to make such an inner conversation more tangible is to write it down in dialogue form. Art decided to do this with Fred, and here's what he came up with:

I'd like to tap into Fred's wisdom. He cares about people, has known tough times, does excellent work, copes with bouts of discouragement. I wonder what he would say to me? I think I'll tell him how I feel.

Art: Fred, I'm really stuck on this job search. I was excited about a possible job offer, but when it fell through, I felt horrible. I know I should keep on talking with people, but all I feel like doing is being alone, working around the yard, and not talking with anyone.

Fred: Yeah, I know how you feel. I've felt that way many times before.

Art: But what have you done about it? How have you bounced back?

Fred: It's not that easy. Sometimes it's like being in a cave — it's dark, and you just can't see light.

Art: Yeah, that's the way I feel now.

Fred: Sometimes you can't DO anything. You just have to wait it out. You're probably doing the best thing you can now — physical labor, getting outside, giving your brain a rest.

Art: Yes, but I feel so useless.

> **Fred:** You might feel that way, but you may be doing something very useful — letting all the thoughts and impressions that have occurred to you during this search percolate a while.
>
> **Art:** I know that can be a good thing to do, that it's important to let things gel, but I still feel useless.
>
> **Fred:** What does that mean to you?
>
> **Art:** Maybe it means that there are other ways to be useful than just concentrating too hard on this search.
>
> **Fred:** Why don't you think about that?

When you set up a dialogue in this fashion, sometimes "new" wisdom or courage is given. Try it once or a few times and see what happens. Here are the steps:

- Become conscious of how you are feeling at this point in your search.
- Think about someone who would understand these feelings and be able to offer wisdom.
- Write a brief description of that person. Why do you want to talk to that person now?
- Imagine the person is with you. Take a few minutes to be conscious of being with the person.
- Then, like Art, begin a written dialogue with the person. Start by describing how you feel right now.
- Be quiet and wait for the response of the other person. Write that down.
- Go back and forth — your reply, the other person's response, until you sense that it is finished.
- Read the dialogue you have written. Add more dialogue if it occurs.
- Add your feelings about what you have written if you wish.

Summarize what was revealed through the dialogue. Put it in the place in your notebook or card file where it is most applicable.

Try this exercise with different kinds of people. Experiment. The sky's the limit. And just think, it doesn't cost a cent. If you don't have time for a full conversation or written dialogue, just call to mind a special person and enjoy their presence. Let them be your inner companion for a while. Whether you write a dialogue or simply think about that other person, you will be enriched by their companionship and perspective.

5

When you're working out a critical strategy, there's nothing like being surrounded by people who want to help and have good ideas.

Carol Van Sickle
"Jobless at 61: A Success Story"[9]

Decide Your Next Move

As you have probably discovered, the help you need, the roles people can fill, and the individuals you can ask — these three angles work together and relate to one another in different ways. Sometimes they come together clearly — as they did with Sally. If Sally had schematized her thinking, it would look like this:

> **Help I need:** someone with whom to review my situation
> **Role I need filled:** friend who will listen
> **Person to ask:** Betty

All this came to her in a flash.

But you know that it doesn't always work that way. You too might be clear about the kind of help you need but unclear about the person to ask. If you, like Sally, want to talk over your situation informally with someone, would you ask your spouse, your parent, a counselor, a friend? Each could offer a listening ear.

You might be clear about the kind of role you need filled, but not about the particular help to ask for. "I'd like to have a spiritual guide. I've heard how important that is. But I'm unclear about exactly what I want from that person."

Or the help you need might be clear, but you may not know any specific individual who could provide it. "At this point, I want advice — should I continue working in this office with the hope that we can make things better or start looking around for another job? I don't know whom to ask about this."

Sometimes one step is clear — and only when you take it will the next become apparent. When Sally first sought advice about personnel work, she had no idea that she would eventually be looking for a good instructor. It was only when her colleague in personnel suggested it that she decided to pursue that route.

As you look over your People Help pages or cards, you will see some actions that seem appropriate to take now to obtain the help you need. Some actions may be left for the future. However, don't be worried if you feel strongly that you need, say, a mentor, but no names come to mind. In naming your desire for a mentor, you have taken an action, and in a sense have created an empty cup.

This is a container to collect ideas or clues related to your wish for a mentor. Watch: It will go with you everywhere. By articulating what you want in this way, you alert your unconscious mind to be on the lookout for appropriate assistance. In time it will come.

 Look over your notebook pages or cards labeled "People Help." Identify next moves to make that seem right for now. Record those moves on cards or in your notebook.

GATHERING

Purpose: *To recognize and enhance your reaching to others for personal support; to share progress on Vocational Exploration Plans and practical parameters you want to change*
Everyone Bring:
Examples of giving and receiving help from Segment 1
People Help pages from Segment 3
Next moves from Segment 5
Vocational Exploration Plan from Chapter 4, Segment 5
Practical parameters to change from Chapter 3, Segment 3

Warm-Up (Everyone)   **25 minutes**

Tell some stories of times when you gave and/or received help that made a real difference. Add examples from people you know about if you have time.

Moving On (Everyone)   **40 minutes**

1.   Each person speak about:
   - helper roles you'd like filled
   - specific help you need
   - next moves you contemplate
2.   Each person ask for encouragement or ideas to help you move forward.
3.   Period of silence for each person to record any insights that will help them move.

Update: (Everyone)   **20 minutes**

1.   Take a minute to review the work you are doing or want to do related to your Vocational Exploration Plan and the practical parameters you want to change.

2.   Each person describe action taken on your Vocational Exploration Plan and the practical parameters you want to change.
3.   Ask for help or affirmation to keep moving.

Closing (Everyone)   **5 minutes**

The important part is not the network, the finished product, but the process of getting there — the communication that creates the linkages between people and clusters of people.

John Naisbitt
Megatrends[10]

Build A Network

Entering her new office, Kate glanced at the bare walls and functional furniture. "This space is dead. I've got to do something with it," she decided. Rather than display her diplomas or teaching certification and other emblems of achievement, she surrounded herself with photos — of her husband, a dear friend, her French teacher, the head of an organization she respected: those who had influenced and encouraged her. Imagine being supported in one's workspace by those who have had a hand in shaping you. It is a most impressive sight.

The new-found companions you have been thinking about join your existing community of allies and guides to form what might be called your "personal network." These are the people who know and care that you develop into the person you want to be. Rejoice in your widening group of resources and linkages. Value what you have, explore new possibilities, build your network.

Now is the time to make your next move. Give a person a call or drop them a note; let a friend know you want to be introduced.

Or draw an empty cup, stating one specific need you have, related to people help, such as, "I need a mentor"; "I need advice on training." Place this on your fridge.

The energy you invest in making these moves will return handsome dividends.

You may be feeling hesitant about asking a particular person for help. If so, consider the following:

- What is the source of your hesitancy? Are there ways to recognize your concerns without letting them get the upper hand?
- Are there intermediary steps you can take before you approach a person for support — perhaps have someone introduce you informally?
- Are there ways to find out about the person before you meet?
- Could someone else who does not make you feel hesitant offer similar assistance?

Most people pause before jumping into the water. When you do jump in, however, chances are you'll discover "the water's fine."

On your Summary Page for this chapter, list the names of specific people or roles you want people to fill to help support your present quest for meaningful work.

6

Feed the Whole Person

We can now understand that the fate of the soul is the fate of the social order, that if the spirit within us withers, so too will all the world we build about us.

Theodore Roszak
Where the Wasteland Ends[1]

Water the Soul

Picture yourself walking along a lonely beach. The sun tips the horizon, swathing the earth in a blaze of color. You are invigorated by brisk wind brushing your face, soothed by the beat of the rolling waves. You walk along and feel at home in a friendly universe.

Scene Two. At a huge outdoor concert, you and hundreds of other fans listen and move to the music of your favorite musical group. Applause and grateful voices pierce the air after every number. You are joyful, filled with emotion as you and the rest of the concert goers respond deeply to the music. You are part of a people uplifted by a common love.

Or another scene. Your father has given you the old careworn table that once belonged to his father. You are in your basement surrounded by turpentine, stain remover, and rags. You are lovingly restoring the cherished table, exploring every crack, remembering where it once stood and how many times members of your family and their friends had gathered around it for meals and celebrations. You feel connected with generations of your forebears and strengthened by their faithful living of life.

In each of these experiences, your life is nourished in ways that defy description. Words, in fact, may take away from such experiences. You know they have happened. You savor their power. Each such experience creates a part of your inner life and leaves you feeling restored, more whole, more at one with yourself and your world.

This "feeding of the whole person" is what you need on a consistent basis if you are to discover and develop work from the heart.

As a Peace Corps volunteer in the Philippines, Ben felt a pull to commit his life to development work among the poor. Having read Dominique Lapierre's *City of Joy*, which describes the work of Polish priest Stephan Kovalski among the desperately poor in Calcutta, Ben realized that he wanted to do something similar. He knew, however, that he wasn't ready to do this work.

He said: "I know that development work among impoverished people is going to take stamina and commitment, and I also know that I'm not there yet. I care about people and feel moved to continue this kind of work, but I don't have the spiritual depth to sustain the long-term commitment I want to make. I need to learn how to refuel on a regular basis so I can weather the times when I will not see results or feel that I'm doing anything worthwhile."

Ben's statement is important. Just as plants and trees require a rhythm of regular nourishment from the air, water, and sun, so you need to find the diet that best feeds your whole being and brings alive on a regular basis the beliefs and values that mean most to you. When that special combination of body, mind, and spirit that is uniquely you is well nourished, you are fully alive and bring your best self to everything you do, including your work or search for work. Further, when you learn specific nourishment practices and habits that are right for you, you can seek illumination or guidance from them, depending on what particular work situations require. A well-thought out program of sustenance is also an important antidote to burn-out — that loss of energy, inspiration, and creativity that plagues so many in relation to their work.

However, it is not always easy to find nourishment that truly builds up your body, mind, and spirit. Organized religion typically has been entrusted with raising consciousness about the importance of such sustenance. But religious institutions can lose sight of this important task. The result is that today many people, including those involved in an organized religion, may be kept busy but find themselves hungry for nourishment that satisfies.

Yet, sometimes all that is needed is an invitation to name and address this hunger. Ask yourself the key question of this chapter:

What ongoing nourishment do I need
to discover and sustain work from the heart?

A good way to begin addressing this question is to build on what you already know about yourself.

When Walt was invited to think about what had nourished him throughout his life, he said that films were important to him. Asked why, he mused a while and then penned these words:

> I shall never forget the first time I saw Ingmar Bergman's film, "Seventh Seal." It was the first art film I had seen. The images haunted me for years. The photography had a powerful effect. I could see how effective film can be in stimulating a person to think deeply about the issues presented. In this case, I pondered the meaning of life and death for months afterwards, still challenged by the ambiguity and depth of Bergman's masterpiece.

Thinking about how much he valued films throughout his life heightened Walt's consciousness about their power for him. He became newly enthusiastic about incorporating films into the classes he teaches — and about exploring how they can fuel the search for meaning.

Think back over your life to times when you felt that your whole being was nourished, lifted, invigorated — you choose the word. List these experiences or activities. Or make a drawing that gives expression to each of them.

Select one and reflect on its significance. What were the circumstances? What did you do? What was inspiring or nurturing about it? Reflect on why the experience was important for you. Ask yourself if there is anything from that experience that you would like to incorporate in your life today. Write whatever comes to you.

After journaling about **The Irrational Season**[2] *by L'Engle, I decided to try her practice of believing seven impossible things before breakfast. I did this during a morning walk, and it led to a series of rich fantasies or stories I participated in — vivid, colorful, wild! I was so energized by this experience.*

Seminar Participant

Thirty-Minute Workout for the Creative Spirit

"Go ahead and play," exclaimed Joan as she handed her friend Dan an inviting lump of clay.

"But I've never worked with ceramics before," Dan protested.

"Don't worry about that," replied Joan. "Just fool around with it for a while, get quiet, begin to let it form itself."

With soft music in the background, Dan closed his eyes, settled himself, and played with the material, tossing it between his hands. It softened with his touch. Rolling it into a ball occurred without any thought — then shaping the ball. "This is sorta fun," Dan mused. "I don't know if anything will come of it, but I sure feel relaxed." Gradually a form emerged. After a few minutes, Dan knew that he had finished what he wanted to make.

Setting his piece on a table, with a gaze of admiration, he exclaimed, "That's amazing! I never knew I could do something like this." Others in the room shared his wonder. The form had taken the shape of a nurturing woman holding a cherished object in her lap.

"That's beautiful!" said one of the others. "It reminds me of mothering."

Dan's wife added, "You know, it depicts how you are with me. You have a wonderful way of holding me and our life together in a calm and strong way." For Dan, this was an "ah hah!" experience — getting in touch with his artistic powers in a fresh and renewing way.

With Mary, a new way to express herself came through an altogether different medium. One day, while pushing her aging father in his wheel chair along the halls of the nursing home, she was surprised by his request. "Mary, I want to coast down the wheel chair ramp — give the chair a shove and let me go!"

Giving him a gentle push, Mary scurried to the bottom of the ramp to receive her father in his free-wheeling ride. She was elated by the exhilarated look on his face.

"That was great, Mary. Let's do it again!"

Suddenly, Mary was aware of how much movement, dance, sliding, skating, and rolling had meant to her father and how many playful hours they had once spent engaging in this nearly forgotten form of fun. Almost simultaneously, she realized how much she too loved movement and how much she missed having more of it in her life.

In planning her next vacation, Mary knew that movement was going to be a big part of it. Taking two weeks, she spent them in Arizona enrolled in a class led by a well known eighty-year-old dancer. That same summer Mary turned sixty. "These wonderful weeks of dance were my birthday present to myself," she said. "It has been a long time since I have felt so deeply refreshed and alive."

What made these experiences so enlivening for Dan and Mary? A number of things. Both exercised aspects of their being that had not received much attention. In a very real sense, these parts of themselves came alive — Dan's artistic ability and Mary's love of movement.

Dan and Mary also tapped their creativity. In a society where spectator sports and television are so prevalent, it is all too possible to lose touch with our own imaginative gifts. Not because they are absent, but because they are not fully exercised. When creativity is expressed, it becomes stronger and links us tangibly with the creative force in all of life.

Creativity is also related to satisfaction in the workplace. When surveyed on what makes work meaningful, many people cite as first choice the desire to "exercise my ingenuity on the job" — and consequently find themselves looking for a job where "my imagination is valued."

What follows is a smorgasbord of activities that cultivate the kind of nourishment that sustains and replenishes creativity. Some will be new, some familiar. Taste a few of them. Savor the various sensations they evoke. Use them to think about what "works" for you.

- **Commune with nature.** In one part of their interview together, Bill Moyers and Joseph Campbell talked about the power they receive from being present to nature:

  > **Moyers:** On my first visit to Kenya, I went alone to one of the ancient sites of a primitive camp on what used to be the shore of a lake, and stayed there until night fell, feeling a sense of the presence of all creation — sensing underneath that night sky, in that vast place, that I belonged to something ancient, something very much still alive.
  >
  > **Campbell:** I think it's Cicero who says that when you go into a great tall grove, the presence of a deity becomes known to you. There are sacred groves everywhere. Going into the forest as a little boy, I can remember worshiping a tree, a great big old tree, thinking, "My, my, what you've known and been." I think this sense of the presence of creation is a basic mood of man. But we live now in a city. It's all stone and rock, manufactured by human hands. It's a different kind of world to grow up in when you're out in the forest with the little chipmunks and the great owls. All these things are around you as presences, representing forces and powers and magical possibilities of life that are not yours and yet are all part of life, and that opens it out to you. Then you find it echoing in yourself, because you are nature. When a Sioux Indian would take the calumet, the pipe, he would hold it up stem to the sky so that the sun could

take the first puff. And then he'd address the four directions always. In that frame of mind, when you're addressing yourself to the horizon, to the world that you're in, then you're in your place in the world. It's a different way to live.[3]

For many people, nature is taken for granted. However, when you pay attention, newness leaps out at you. Take trees. How many times have you admired them? Try focusing your attention on just one tree. Now address the tree: "I am open to your wisdom." Listen to what is given.

Or: Take a few minutes to lie on the ground. Feel the earth support you, notice the sky above. These words from Big Thunder speak of earth power:

> The Great Spirit is our father, but the earth is our mother. She nourishes us; that which we put into the ground she returns to us, and healing plants she gives us likewise. If we are wounded, we go to our mother and seek to lay the wounded part against her, to be healed.[4]

Experience the reality of Big Thunder's words as you are being held by Mother Earth.

- **Build an altar.** This is a time-honored way of communing with powers beyond the ordinary. Altar building can take so many forms — a candle invites focus, nature objects point to the variety, fecundity, and intricacy of the created order. Altar building can be done alone or with other people. Try it. Experiment. Receive power beyond the ordinary.

Today is my mother-in-law's birthday — she would have been 81. It is a day to honor her spirit and let it feed my own. I place her photo where we will see it in the dining room. Before it I place a paint brush and pen, reminders of her artistic and literary talent. Behind the table on which these objects lie, I hang a watercolor of a church, one of our favorite paintings created by Mom. In the low vase with flowers, already on the table, I notice previously collected rocks arranged to hold the few blooms upright. They remind me of Mom's love of stone wall building.

In these few minutes — no more than five — I am reminded of and enhanced by Mom's strength and gifts. I am made larger and more wealthy by this communion with another soul.

- **Write a poem.** The arrangement of words artistically on a page can infuse them with new meaning. Choosing phrases to express precisely how you feel forces a distillation that in turn presses more meaning into each word chosen. That is poetry. There is no right way to create poetry.

What matters

is that

you feel your feelings deeply,

think your thoughts clearly,.

choose your words carefully,

arrange them artfully.

Get the idea? Try it.

- **Cultivate the outlaw part of yourself.** The movie title "Breaking Away" vividly describes the drive to move beyond the confining boxes that trap us. What boxes? The ones that say, "I can't do anything different or new" or "It's always been like this." In stating her hopes for joining our seminar, Nan said:

> I hope to be bigger —
> to have bigger dreams,
> bigger goals and expectations,
> bigger willingness to risk,
> bigger self-esteem and appreciation
> of my possibilities and to have
> a bigger life with God.

To become bigger, we need to break away from old understandings of ourselves and the world. James Fowler and Sam Keen in *Life Maps* invite us to become outlaws. "The Outlaw stage begins with a crime, the killing of the old authorities."[5]

Feminist leader Gloria Steinem, in an address to students at a midwestern college, challenged them to be different, think different, act different. She told them if they could not do it now in college, they might never be able to do it. She then urged them to do one outrageous act for simple justice in the next twenty-four hours.

Take her advice: Express the outlaw in yourself:

- Do one outrageous act for simple justice.
- Speak out about something that's been bugging you.
- Give up one "duty" you planned on doing this week and use the time to do something that challenges the status quo.

The word mystical derives from the Greek mystos, "keeping silence." Mystical experience reveals phenomena that are usually silent and inexplicable. This expanded consciousness, this whole-knowing, transcends our limited powers of description. Sensation, perception, and intuition seem to merge to create something that is none of these.

Marilyn Ferguson
The Aquarian Conspiracy[6]

Be Open to Mystery and Transcendence

Alone in the woods, the Indian brave is on his vision quest. It is a time of major transition. He leaves the tribe a boy and returns a man. Without food or shelter, confronted by his weakness, he must conjure up strength to survive. He seeks a totem — an animal, an element of nature, a geological object — with which to identify. Caught in a furious storm, his body shakes with the roar of clapping thunder. Then, suddenly, he experiences a radically different sensation. The energy and power of the thunder becomes an inspiration and reminds him that he has the energy and power to find his way.

Seeking shelter under a rock, he sleeps peacefully. The next morning he locates roots that assuage his hunger, enabling him to make his way back to the village. Walking triumphantly to the chief, he announces his new name — "Great Thunder."

What happened in this vision quest to change the frightened youngster into tall-standing Great Thunder? The answer lies in the realm of the indescribable. It is what spiritual writers grope for as they picture a mystic moving from the stages of Purgation (emptying of false desires) to Illumination (having a vision of the good) to Union (being infused by the good).

The young brave emptied himself of the easy childhood security provided by tribal life and received illumination from the phenomenon of thunder. But then something much more startling occurred: He became one with the thunder. The power of the thunder was transferred to him, and he BECAME Great Thunder.

However sublime and impossible to describe, this experience is akin to something as simple as eating an apple. As you consume an apple, its energy is transferred to you. The apple is in you, and through the process of digestion, you receive energy from it.

Can we reproduce the conditions of the vision quest in our overcrowded lives, and more important, can we guarantee that an infusion of power and clarity will occur? We can try to replicate the conditions, but we cannot guarantee results. The very nature of the vision quest is to venture into the unknown. Yet if we are open to receiving energy, power, and guidance from contact with mystery and transcendence, there is an excellent chance that this intention on our part will be rewarded.

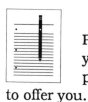 Put on a tape of your favorite music. Relax and let it fill you with its power. Open yourself to it as completely as possible. Let it fill your whole being. Receive what it has to offer you.

Sit quietly for a time and receive any image, word, or sense of transcendent power that may be given.

It is important to do this exercise without specific expectation. A sense of "oughtness" can block the glimpses of what may be given. Whatever happens, value your own willingness to be open to new experience. It may take time before you feel a sense of that which is beyond your rational processes.

When you have finished, rest a few minutes and absorb what has happened. Record anything that seems important.

As another way of getting into this mode of "being," set aside a half hour of time, sit quietly and try to recall any time in your life when you have experienced a sense of union or connection with the transcendent — when you had a true feeling of unity with that which is beyond yourself. Make a few notes in your journal about these experiences and their meaning for you.

Don't press yourself to come up with something. It may be more important simply to sit quietly, to give yourself the opportunity to receive that which you cannot describe. Cultivating an attitude of receptivity and openness is the foundation for experiences of what lies beyond your own knowledge.

The central concern of spirituality is fullness of life. Since the only life we know is earthly and sensual, it follows that this is the stuff of our spirituality. Hence, even such things as running and jumping and skiing and swimming can become part of our language with God. The challenge of any spirituality is to integrate all the aspects of life in our engagement with the world. We arrive at wholeness by using to the fullest the stuff of our human experience, rather than by denying or diminishing it or seeing it as outside the pale of our relationship with God.

Thomas Ryan
Wellness, Spirituality, and Sports[7]

Finding What Works for You

All of her life, Evelyn was a voracious reader. She had always been nourished by books, all kinds of books. But she began to realize that the written word was having less and less appeal for her. "I feel flooded with words," she said. "Junk mail, newspapers, speeches, articles, words — spoken and written. I'm sick of verbiage. Spiritual nourishment has to be life-giving if it really is going to work. I'm beginning to crave nonverbal forms of replenishment."

Evelyn started walking daily, appreciating the seasonal changes. This heightened her love for the earth. She began to turn more to gardening, then to clay modeling. One thing led to another. She even treated herself to a desert visit in solitude, as a break from her busy east coast, surburban life, and realized how much that landscape fed her. Each of these activities revitalized her commitment to her work as a legislative advocate.

Use Evelyn's word "life-giving" as a litmus test for whatever ways you choose to nourish your being or touch the transcendent. Allow your gut responses to lead you to fresh experiences. Build contrast into your life — verbal/nonverbal, suburb/desert, solitude/community, head/heart.

In a college alumni magazine, a reader wrote, "I have learned that I want to give my children roots and wings — a tie to the traditional and a lift toward the new." Think about your need for both roots and wings as you choose ways to nourish the deepest parts of yourself.

Sarah, for example, routinely and regularly reads a bit of sacred writing from one of the great religious traditions of the world. "This grounds me in ancient wisdom," she says. "But in addition to that, I also love to read current books that are pushing and integrating the frontiers of knowledge."

Body, mind, and spirit. Feed all the parts of yourself. Perhaps, like Evelyn, you will have long periods when you focus on one or the other. Or you may want to strike a balance among the three.

In addition to body, mind, and spirit, there are different "persons" within the one person you call yourself. Todd shared how this was for him: "In me there is a village elder who wants to be settled in the center of town and be in the middle of things. But there also is a wanderer who loves to travel and explore new places. I've learned that I have to feed both the village elder and the wanderer in me."

Nourishing your whole being involves receiving the insight, energy, and techniques of others, as well as conceiving your own ideas, images, and practices. Thus, at galleries, Linda drinks in the art of the masters, but at home draws or paints images that come from within herself. Reading the wisdom of others can be complemented by writing about the insights you gain personally through experience.

Here is a way to chart the processes of receiving and conceiving:

Receiving	**Conceiving**
• reading the thoughts of others	• writing your own thoughts in a notebook
• learning the wisdom of the ages	• personal wisdom gained through own experience
• viewing other people's art	• creating own art
• watching sports	• involvement in sports
• seeing others' gardens	• making own garden

Nourishment, for some people, relates very specifically to daily work. Meg is such a person. Whenever she travels, she visits special gardens created by others. She also learns from others through courses and reading in ecology and conservation. Her own creativity is expressed through gardening and the journal writing of her musings on these subjects. All of this feeds her work as a state leader in wildflower preservation.

For other people, a contrast between work and inner nourishment practices is important. Ted loves disengaging his mind on weekends, puttering in the garden and yard, and being by himself. This renews him for his highly interactive, fast-moving management job during the week.

The most important consideration is what works and is life-giving for you.

What kinds of inner nourishment are life-giving for you? For each thing you think of, write notes to yourself in response to these questions:

- How am I incorporating this into my life now?
- What effect is this having on my life?
- How would I like to incorporate this in the future?

I begin each day with 15 minutes of silent, alone time. This is important for two reasons. First, I want to change the way I begin each day. I want to begin it with welcome and appreciation rather than with resistance. Second, I want to begin to establish a regular rhythm of "sacred time."

Seminar participant

Create a Way to Continue

It is one thing to have an occasional illuminating experience, such as a walk in a beautiful forest or a night out absorbing a well-crafted play. It is quite another to build into your life regular periods of nourishment that provide the ongoing energy and guidance you need to live life fully.

People who want to keep in good physical shape know the importance of regular involvement in physical activity. But they go about it in different ways. An avid tennis player, Judy focuses on that sport almost exclusively. She does stretching exercises and some running, but all toward the goal of improving her tennis game. She is a "planner" and schedules her games and exercise periods regularly for each week.

Nick, equally enthusiastic about physical conditioning, goes about it quite differently. In his garage is a bike, some skis, a tennis racket, and garden tools. Outside is a canoe. Everything is on hand. On a given day, depending on the weather and his other commitments, he can create in the moment the kind of physical conditioning that is right for that day. Nick thrives on being a spontaneous person. He surrounds himself with possibilities, and then chooses in the moment what he will do.

Are you a planner or an "in-the-moment" person? Select the activity which suits you best.

- **Activity for Planners**

Look over what you have written in your notebook or on cards for this chapter. Review the nourishing experiences you have valued in the past and new ideas that have come to you. Which of these experiences would you like to schedule regularly into your life? Choose four.

Then with colored markers or pens, draw these in your notebook or on cards as the "four posts" that will support a nourishing lifestyle. Include a statement about how frequently you will engage in each experience. Call this your Nourishment Plan and bring it to share during the Gathering session.

- **Activity for In-the-Moment People**

Look over what you have written in your notebook or on cards for this chapter. Choose the categories of experience you believe will be most nourishing to you in the next period of your life. Create spaces in your home where you can place the materials/equipment necessary for these activities — for example, a shelf of art materials in your closet, sports equipment in your basement, favorite reading in your living room. Create pockets of space in your week that are reserved for this nourishment. During those times, take part in the selected activity that will be most life-giving in the moment.

Describe or draw the arrangements you have made for regular nourishment and call it your Marketplace of Possibilities. Bring this to share in the Gathering session.

GATHERING

Purpose: *To encourage your desire for inner nourishment by sharing and learning from others*
Leaders Bring: *newsprint, magic markers*
Everyone Bring:
List of nourishing experiences from Segment 1
Nourishment Plan or Marketplace of Possibilities from Segment 5

Warm-Up (Everyone)   **20 minutes**
1. What's worked well?
Describe one experience of inner nourishment in your life that has been particularly good (from Segment 1).

2. New ideas to try
What new ideas for inner nourishment have you tried or would you like to try?

Support and Feedback (Four's)   **45 minutes**
1.   Share your Nourishment Plan or Marketplace of Possibilities. Ask for feedback based on the following questions (30 minutes):
     • Is it realistic?
     • Is it balanced?
     • Is it energizing?
2.   Think about how the inner nourishment you want to build into your life relates to the work you do. Have some fun discussing this (15 minutes).

Moving On (Two's)   **5 minutes**
Agree to be each other's "patrons" (see definition in Chapter 5, Segment 2). Make plans to contact each other weekly for the next month to check on how nourishment is happening in your lives.

Encouragement Huddle (Everyone)   **15 minutes**

Put some newsprint on the floor with lots of markers. Huddle around and write the most encouraging words you can think of that will send you off in good spirits to live a more fully nourished life this week. Have some laughs, share the words, illustrate with a drawing or two.

Closing (Everyone)   **5 minutes**

7

The first, easiest and most obvious assistance toward an individual's private efforts is the simple association with others making the same attempt.

Anonymous

Weighing In

Few people doubt the value of the life-enhancing experiences and practices described in the foregoing pages. The challenge is to build them into your life in fruitful ways, to tend your whole being through establishing health-producing habits. Like other life-giving practices, however, no matter how much you know you want to do them, it helps a great deal to have someone who cares and a method of checking progress.

"I know I should eat right, but what keeps me faithful is regular attendance at Weight Watchers," said Mark. When asked what makes the program work for him, he replied: "Two things. Support and check-ins. I go with a friend who cares about my progress, and each night I attend my weight is checked. My progress, or lack of progress, is tracked."

Mark put his finger on two ways to reinforce your desire to nourish your whole being. It helps a great deal to have someone who cares and a method of checking progress. This may involve something as simple as responding in a weekly phone call or over lunch to the question, "How are you doing?" Or it may entail meeting with like-minded people who choose certain practices in common and provide group energy to support each one in doing them.

Don't let your nourishment practices go stale. Ask yourself: Is my routine "life-giving"? Does it "work"? Is there enough freshness as well as stability? Be honest with yourself as you think about these questions. What works well for one person may be deadly for another. Although we have touched on the sacred in what we've been describing, there are no sacred cows.

Experiment. Find what most enlivens you and feeds your creativity. Build life-giving nourishment experiences into your life. It's a wonderful investment of time and helps immeasurably in the quest for "work from the heart."

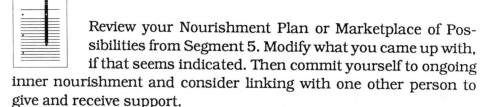 Review your Nourishment Plan or Marketplace of Possibilities from Segment 5. Modify what you came up with, if that seems indicated. Then commit yourself to ongoing inner nourishment and consider linking with one other person to give and receive support.

Choose something that you can carry in your pocket or purse as a symbol of what is nourishing to you. As you touch it throughout the day, let it serve as a reminder of what feeds your whole self. It might be a shell that reminds you of freedom or a stone that calls you to integrity. Allow your symbol to influence how you go about your work.

On the Summary Page for this chapter, record the Nourishment Plan or Marketplace of Possibilities you are committed to for the next period of time.

7

Consider Your Environment

Those who believe in dignity, meaning and community and who want to create the . . . best place to work must somehow, someway involve everybody.

Marvin R. Weisbord
Productive Workplaces[1]

The Where in What We Do

The Madeira School, an independent high school for young women, sits perched on a cliff high above the Potomac River. Far below, one's eye is held by the boiling rapids at Difficult Run. Since 1906, Madeira has been an educational leader known for its active, interested faculty and lively, intelligent student body. It was without hesitation that we accepted the school's invitation to help out with a pre-opening orientation for its student leaders.

When the appointed day came, we stood before the young women and asked simply, "What type of school do you want to create this year?" With little prompting, their thoughts on the subject tumbled out filling the room with a spirit of hope. Their answers were illuminating. They captured what we all crave in a workplace:

> "UNITY but also respect for INDIVIDUAL DIVERSITY, where we can have PRIDE in ourselves, our work, and our school."

In an hour's time, these teenagers pinned down the characteristics their school needed to have in order to sustain and develop work from the heart. Intuitively, they knew a basic truth: **No matter how motivated an individual is to do an excellent job, if the work environment is not organized to support that motivation, the worker becomes less creative, more dispirited and ultimately less productive.**

Your own experience will give you ample evidence of this truth. There have been times when your workplace or one that you know about has been supportive — people were fairly paid, there was a good spirit among the workers, the work itself was worthwhile. You have also known bad situations — where performance was not fairly evaluated, compensation was not up to snuff, the workspace itself was unattractive or inefficient. In the former, you labor with ease, and your product is a thing of quality. In the latter, you chafe and buck, and find yourself longing for a change.

The key question for this chapter is:

How can my work environment foster work from the heart?

Unlike the other topics in this book, creating a supportive work place depends on the actions of others in addition to your own effort or resolve. This chapter's purpose is to raise issues and incite reaction. It will help you become more conscious of what constitutes a supportive workplace for you and what you can or cannot do to create it.

Reflect back on your experiencesand observations of the workplace. Describe in a short paragraph one time you felt a work environment was empowering and one time you felt it was squelching. Now draw two columns and list at least five characteristics of an empowering workplace and five characteristics of a squelching one.

Only a company with a real mission or sense of purpose that comes out of an intuitive or spiritual dimension will capture people's hearts. And you must have people's hearts to inspire the hard work required to realize a vision.

John Naisbitt and Patricia Aburdene
Re-Inventing the Corporation[2]

The Monday Morning Guide to Where You'd Rather Work

A number of recent books have attempted to answer the question, "What does an organization look like that supports work from the heart?" Labor and business reporter Robert Levering went on a hunt for America's "superlative employers," and with others catalogued them in *The 100 Best Companies to Work for in America.* Approaching the question from a management perspective, consultants Thomas Peters and Robert Waterman in *In Search of Excellence* analyzed some of the best-run companies in America and discovered "action-stimulating, people-oriented, profit-maximizing practices"[3] that are readily transferable to other settings. Building on this work, John Naisbitt and Patricia Aburdene, in *Re-Inventing the Corporation,* set themselves the task of envisioning the corporate role in society based on current trends.

Although the insights and examples offered by these thinkers relate to companies, they can be adapted in other institutions such as schools, community organizations, and faith communities. This is what some of their key ideas look like when grouped under "work from the heart" headings. While reading these descriptions, note those points that are particularly relevant to you.

GIFTS

Work from the heart involves doing what you love and taking pride in a good job well done. The supportive workplace should help you do precisely that.

Naisbitt and Aburdene say that many people today believe that work should be fulfilling — and even fun. This translates into corporate practices such as putting people in charge of the work they do, tracking and rewarding results, emphasizing quality and excellence in performance, and making room for the mavericks, whose ideas may challenge the bureaucracy, but ultimately benefit the customer.

MEANING

Work from the heart incorporates values most important to you. The supportive workplace is concerned with individual and corporate values.

People want their organizations to have a sense of social responsibility. Schools must not simply teach the three R's, but also include character education and back that up with community service programs. People are asking their faith communities to do justice, not simply talk about it. Corporations must not only give money to service organizations in which employees participate, but produce products and services that make a positive difference in the world.

Organizations in which members can wed meaning and vocation are guided by powerful visions: a sense of where they are going and how they will get there. This vision can be created at the top by the leader or can be forged by groups of people — such as the Madeira students mentioned in Segment 1, who want to participate in creating the vision.

When your personal sense of mission coincides with your organization's vision, there is a sense of alignment and momentum that gives purpose to the work you do. Naisbitt and Aburdene describe vision as "the link between dream and action." When you envision the future you want, they say, "you can more easily achieve your goal."[4]

PARAMETERS

Work from the heart includes serious consideration of practical parameters. The supportive workplace takes into account givens in your life.

Recognizing the interconnectedness of life, companies, universities, and religious organizations are organizing more child care facilities, offering backup help for members with elderly parents, investing in local school improvement, establishing medical programs for ill employees, providing wellness programs to keep people in top condition, and installing flexible working arrangements such as flex time and job sharing.

The school, religious community, or company that gives attention to the practical issues people have outside the organization's scope of work draws more committed, fuller participation.

FOCUS

Work from the heart applies your talents and vision to a specific task. The supportive workplace organizes tasks so that each one's talents are used, their vision is honored, and these are focused toward a result worth achieving.

Listen to this fantasy written by organization consultant Tom Dunne about the wise old man who helped some women and men think about "Good Work":

> A great silence came over the group. The old man leaned forward, and this is what he said: "To be human is to long to do Good Work."
>
> The group sat in stunned silence. Indeed, something stirred in each of their hearts, and yet the meaning of his words was still a mystery. "What," they asked, "is 'Good Work?' "
>
> The old man spoke again: "Think, please, of the time in each of your lives when you were happiest in your work. What was it like?"
>
> There was a pause. Some of the managers closed their eyes as they remembered. Happiness came to their faces. And then someone said: "I knew what I was supposed to do, and it was something important." And another, "I could see the results of my work."
>
> A third added: "When I discovered better ways to do my work, I could make those improvements."
>
> And so it continued, until the leaders had made a long list.

RESEARCH, TRAINING, EXPERIENCE

Work from the heart is supported in an ongoing way through research, training, and experience. The supportive workplace encourages you to do research, undergo training, and seek out broadening experiences that will help you grow.

An important question for many people who go to work in an organization is, "What will I learn?" According to Levering, great companies "expand the skills of its people through training programs and reimbursement of tuition for outside courses."[5]

PERSONAL SUPPORT
Work from the heart involves giving and receiving personal support along the way. Supportive workplaces increasingly see that the best response to the question, "Who is there for me?" is, "WE ALL ARE!"

Hierarchical ways of organizing institutions are being replaced by more cooperative structures that result in the feeling, "We are all in this together." Teamwork, self-management, small autonomous working groups, open communication foster a "we" approach to getting things done rather than a "we/they" split.

INNER NOURISHMENT
Work from the heart is sustained by a nourishing lifestyle. The supportive workplace provides opportunities for all parts of you — body, mind and spirit — to be fed.

Plants and trees, art, colorful decor, creative architecture all contribute an ambience that lifts people's spirits and encourages them to do quality work. Sabbaticals offer a change of scene, opportunity for research and study, contact with colleagues, and often travel — all of which give people fresh energy and insight into their work.

The above summary is, of course, only a sampling of ways in which the workplace can support each person's best effort. As you think of your own situation, begin to form a more specific picture of the kind of work environment that best fosters your most productive labor. To help bring that vision into reality may involve attempts to change the environment in which you now work, or attempts to determine the environment in which you will work in the future.

Look back at the foregoing descriptions of supportive work environments. List on a card or in your notebook the items that matter most to you — that would motivate you to offer your best effort. Now write a paragraph that sums up what you are looking for in a work environment. This statement should be an expression of your ideal workplace. Draw a picture of your dream workplace, if you like.

3

I like the way my new job incorporates my abilities and my expertise. I hope that over time there will be ways to incorporate some ideas I have about improving the way our office team works.

Seminar participant

The Hand You've Been Dealt: Assessing Your Workplace

Organizations that support good work have attitudes, activities, and an atmosphere that enable people to:

- offer talents they enjoy using;
- contribute something positive to the world;
- attend to personal and practical concerns;
- produce a product or service that is worthy of pride;
- grow personally and professionally;
- work as a member of a team;
- nourish themselves as whole people.

That's a tall order. But the good news is that this is already occurring in companies, government agencies, and churches around the nation and is likely to happen in many more. You can help it happen in your place of work by recognizing and affirming conditions which enable satisfying work and by changing conditions that stifle your best efforts.

The first step is assessment. What is positive about your workplace, what needs changing, what is unlikely to change?

"How do you like your new job?" Pam was asked about three months after starting as a recreation therapist at a rehabilitation hospital. "The other staff people are very nice," she said. "The facility is fine — we have all the equipment we need. I like my patients and my particular work. But one thing bothers me. My supervisor put off my first evaluation until after I had been here for three months, and then when we met, it was so short a time. I had saved up a bunch of questions about how I am doing and just didn't get a chance to ask them." Pam identified some things she appreciates about her job and one thing she would like to change.

Many people think that Jack's home-based office must be the ideal workplace. In so many ways it is. Situated in the woods, it has a wonderful peaceful atmosphere, is a short commute for his colleagues, and, of course, involves no commute for him. Office furnishings are adequate. His computer, however, is on an old dining room table. His chair, fresh from a garage sale, made his back ache. "I've got to do something about this," Jack exclaimed.

In looking for a job in city management, Henry came to some clarity about what mattered most to him in his work environment: "I know I want to work with people I enjoy. That will be one of the first things I'll look for when I interview. Also I'd like to have a job that doesn't keep me at a desk all day long. I'll be looking to see how much those who interview me expect me to be in the office and how much they want me to be 'out and about' the town. Because I'm single, money isn't as important to me as it is to some people."

Each of these people — Pam, Jack, and Henry — knows that any one workplace can't be ideal, but they are clear about what matters most. Pam and Jack, already employed, have focused on what they like and what they want to change in their work environment, whereas Henry knows what he is looking for.

Reread your statement from Segment 2 on the ideal workplace. If you are currently employed, ground that ideal in the reality of your present job. If you are exploring a focus or searching for work, become more specific about the kind of work environment you envision.

First, review the seven characteristics of a supportive workplace offered in this segment. Then, for each characteristic, write a frank assessment of the place you work — its successes and its failures; or, if you are looking for work, describe your imagined work place in terms of each characteristic. Pay particular attention to those factors that matter most to you, as noted in your statement from Segment 2.

One of the main challenges . . . before every organization [including the church] is to free people in the organization to use their gifts best, to see that real progress . . . depends on the enthusiastic participation of all people, and to recognize people for their accomplishments.

Daniel V. Biles
"Pursuing Excellence in Ministry"[6]

The Power of a Pat on the Back

Supportive practices in the workplace are wonderful to experience. When they are in place, we should make the effort to commend the people responsible for instituting them.

In most work groups, there are performance evaluations for individuals — managers, support people, teachers, students, religious leaders. These are generally functional and a scheduled part of the institutional routine. But evaluations don't have to be like that. In his latest book, *A Great Place to Work*, Robert Levering describes the most unusual form of recognition he has ever come across — the "you done GOOD" award.[7] Any employee can send it to any other employee. Here it is — specific, participatory, upbeat:

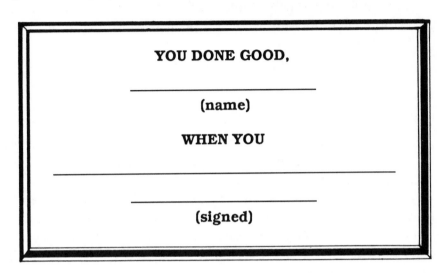

It is all too easy to complain about what is wrong with a work situation and to take for granted what is good. Yet, when you affirm the positive, further positive actions usually occur. When the dean of a local college sent a questionnaire to all staff asking about their needs for a child care facility on campus, many respondents not only filled out the form, but added a note of thanks to the administrator for caring about their family needs. The dean was delighted and doubled her commitment to providing quality child care for her staff.

As Monica served meals in the shelter for the homeless where she works, she was weighed down by the drab look of the place. "This place needs a face lift," she thought. When she shared this observation with one of her artist friends, the painter offered to donate some paintings for the walls. Sparked by this contribution, Monica called other artists and soon filled the common rooms of the shelter with colorful works of art. "Wow, what a difference!" exclaimed one of the residents.

Several residents decided to invite the artists to share a meal with them in their newly decorated dining room. Seeing how appreciative the residents were, the artists began to organize an "art for the homeless" project whose aim was to donate art pieces to all the shelters in their city.

Affirmation of the good someone does is valuable in itself. It often has a ripple effect as well, in which positive actions are multiplied.

 Review your workplace assessment from Segment 3. Pick out a handful of people who are responsible for a brighter, better, more empowering workplace and drop them a note or send them a You Done Good Award.

If you are still in search of work, note in your daily travels three workplaces where an "angel's" hand is in evidence — where good work is done with an upbeat spirit. How are these places supporting work from the heart? What would you say to the "angel" in a thank you note if you worked in that environment?

If you want to move a company or some other kind of institution in a new direction, people within that institution must share a sense of that direction . . . . For best results, the people in the institution must have "ownership" in the new vision . . . . [More] and more these decisions will be made from the bottom up in a participatory fashion . . .

John Naisbitt
Megatrends[8]

 ## The Powerful Act of Making Change

"If I listed everything I'd change at work, it would rival Plato's collected works in length," lamented Arnold, an assistant professor of philosophy at a major university.

"The status quo seems a monolith, against which I am impotent. What can I do?"

Change is the process of directing an already moving chain of events. In all cases it involves three simple steps:

- picturing where you want to go;
- articulating and executing tasks that will take you there;
- making mid-course corrections.

It is as if you were adrift at sea. Even if you sat perfectly still making not a move to control the vessel, you would still be moving. To reach a destination, you need to spot your objective — a small island perhaps — trim the sails, and then continually relocate your destination, and make fine adjustments in your rudder and sail positions.

In the workplace, an accurate, inspiring vision of what a supportive work environment would look like is the first step toward change. When Arnold thought about it, he realized his negative feelings about work were a jumble of complaints that weighed him down but didn't really lead toward change. He asked himself this question, "What one change would really lift my spirits and help me believe that my work matters?" After some thought, this is what he came up with:

> We teach philosophy to students but never talk about it among ourselves as faculty. I'd like to converse with my colleagues about what currently excites us in philosophy, how it impacts our lives, and what difference it makes in the world.

Once Arnold had articulated a change he wanted, he still felt discouraged. "I'm low man on the tenure pole," he said. "What good is a vision if I don't have the power to make the changes I want to make?"

Let's look at the issue of change more closely. There are three basic ways to help change happen in an organization. You can unilaterally change the things over which you have power. You can create change in concert with fellow employees. Or you can appeal — alone or with colleagues — to those who have the power to bring the needed change into existence.

As founder and head of W. L. Gore & Associates, Bill Gore was in a good position to make unilateral change. He envisioned a "profitable company where he could recreate the sense of excitement and commitment he had felt as a member of a small task force at the research labs of E. I. Du Pont de Nemours." He wondered why entire companies couldn't be run in the same way as the task force, which "was exciting, challenging, and loads of fun."

Today Bill's company is built around voluntary commitments. It has "no titles, no bosses, no map of managerial authority, and only two objectives: to make money and to have fun."[9]

As a newly hired manager of a retail grocery store, Larry had excellent ideas about hiring refugees ambitious for a fresh start. But the owners resisted. For the time being, Larry must settle for changing those things for which he alone is responsible: organizing a well-run store, being resourceful and accessible to customers and employees, and setting a tone of easygoing informality by his caring warm approach.

Impetus for positive change can occur when people band together. State Department employees, in the midst of important foreign policy decisions, felt the need to rub elbows with key decision makers and international thinkers. So they instituted the "Brown Bag Forum," a weekly lunch, open to all department personnel, where well-known speakers articulate their policy views and open the floor to vigorous challenge and discussion.

Finally, change can occur by appeal to the powers that be. Helga, during an appointment with the principal of her school, suggested that office keys be issued to the faculty, so that they could mimeograph assignments after hours and avoid the daily morning rush. The principal quickly agreed, complimenting Helga on her involvement in the school and her willingness to help it improve.

Return now to Arnold, the professor who felt powerless. He could begin talking about his wish to discuss philosophy with his colleagues to see who else is interested. Perhaps the head of the department feels the way he does; or some of his peers. Or is Arnold the only one? If others are interested, he could form a group to brainstorm ways to fulfill their desire for more intellectual and personal stimulation at work. That way he'd have the encouragement he needs and perhaps be able to bring more to a seemingly impoverished working situation. If no one at work responds to his ideas, he could consider informally gathering philosophy professionals outside the department. That, in itself, might cause Arnold to feel more refreshed and motivated at work. Whatever path Arnold chooses, change has begun.

 Reread your description of the ideal workplace and think about how you might bring your own workplace closer to that ideal. Review your assessment of your current work situation from Segment 3. Pick out one significant but do-able change you want to see happen. Consider whether this change is something to undertake unilaterally, with others, or by appeal. Write down the change you want to see happen and the steps you could take to bring it about.

If you are looking for work, come to the Gathering session with any ideas you have about helping change happen. Jot them down now for ready reference.

GATHERING

Purpose: *To share and discuss how work environments can and should support work from the heart; to consider how you can help realize these conditions or can look for them in a place of future employment*
Leaders Bring: *newsprint, magic markers*
Everyone Bring:
Your written work from Segments 1, 2, 3, 4, and 5

Warm-Up (Everyone)   15 minutes

1. Pop-corn ways in which work environments you know have either enabled or stifled work from the heart (refer to the work you did for Segment 1).

2.   Tell a few stories about pats on the back you have given or are thinking about giving (refer to the work you did for Segment 4).

Support and Encouragement (Three's)   40 minutes

What Really Matters
1.   Each person share list of work characteristics that matter to you (Segment 2) and the assessment of your present or imagined workplace related to these characteristics (Segment 3).
2.   Talk together about what matters most.

How Can I Make a Difference?
1.   Share work done for Segment 5 describing steps for possible change and any jottings of ideas for change.
2.   Ask for encouragement and critique.

Experience and Affirmation (Everyone)   **30 minutes**

1. Share reflections on the possibilities for and obstacles to enabling change:
   - experiences of when you have seen change happen in workplaces and the steps that were involved;
   - experiences of when you have seen change thwarted in workplaces and possible alternative ways the situation(s) could have been handled.
2. Popcorn (and put on newsprint if you wish) words and phrases that will encourage you to bring about change in the workplace, either presently or in the future.

Closing (Everyone)   **5 minutes**

Every demand is met and matched by an appropriate energy. There seems to be nothing I can do to make this happen. I can only be alert to the current and make sure to ride it when it does happen.

Anne Truitt
Daybook[10]

The Serendipity of Change

In deciding whether there is potential for change or action in an organization, consultant Marvin Weisbord asks three questions:

1. Is there a leader willing to take risks for change?

2. Is there a business opportunity crying to be met?

3. Are there people energized to do things differently?[11]

Lucky is the organization that has all three in place. If you're in such a place, your suggestions for change are likely to be welcomed.

But if the time does not seem right for change, take heart — things do not remain static. Bosses are replaced, companies are reorganized, people are moved.

This chapter has encouraged you in the words of Mary Caroline Richards "to behave imaginatively, to envision what is needed, and eventually to create what is not yet present."[12] You have a purse or a daypack full of useful items to take out when you need them and when the time is right. You've set up one-half of the equation for change. You are prepared. The other half will come when you least expect it. It's as if you stand up on a dark night and shout into the distance, "I am ready!" You don't know when that message will be heard by someone now unknown to you, who will answer, "So am I!"

On your Summary Page for this chapter, write the characteristics of the workplace that call forth the best in you.

The process of personal or organizational change is marked by working hard and letting go. You have worked hard to raise your consciousness and perhaps to institute change. Now let go and let events take their course for a while. Practice letting go by engaging in one of your favorite relaxing activities and enjoy.

8 What's Next?

We ain't what we oughta be
we ain't what we wanna be
we ain't what we gonna be
but thank God
we ain't what we was

Anonymous

Take a Look at Where You've Come

Two people hike along a mountain trail. One says, "Let's take a break and soak in the view." Perched on a granite outcropping, they survey the scene — the village below, and then the forest, the surrounding peaks, the sky, and a ribbon of water winding its way through the valley. "What a panorama!" says one. "Yeah, and look how far we've come!" exclaims the other.

After a few moments, one says, "Let's check our bearings." Pulling out a map, they look at where they've come and then chart the next leg of their journey. Finally, getting up and stretching, one says, "OK, time to get moving."

You've been on a journey of vocational exploration. Now as you come to the end of your guided tour, it is time to take a look at all you've done, to rejoice in the progress you've made, and then to consider the key question:

What is my next move?

Think for a minute about the initiatives you have taken: You've uncovered inner resources and asked yourself what matters to you in your work. You've identified what gives you joy as well as what is meaningful. You've thought about, and perhaps talked with, people who can help you along your path, people who care about the things you care about and are prepared to offer a hand. You've considered and touched the deeper dimensions of life and opened yourself to power beyond your own. You've engaged many parts of yourself — your creativity, your commitment, your brain, your heart, and most certainly your feet!

You've glimpsed the stories of people who, as Studs Terkel put it, "hunger for beauty, meaning and a sense of pride"[1] in what they do. You have learned how they overcame obstacles to find or create work that matches their heart values. These people are kindred spirits. Not only are you in good company, you are part of a wider effort.

Having sown all those seeds, you will reap positive results. Some you can name right now. Some will become apparent later. Watch for the ripple effect — you talk with a person now, time goes by, and you meet again, only this time the connection leads to a beautiful breakthrough. Give yourself a moment to rejoice in all that your creative activity has set in motion. Trust that good things will come from it.

 To get a sense of the progress you've made, review the written work you have produced — the statements, the action plans, and the Summary Pages you created for the end of each chapter.

Take this opportunity to make any changes necessary to update the Summary Pages. Then arrange them on a table top or on the floor and let the total picture of what you've learned affect you.

Notice the clarities you have and the commitments you want to make as you continue to develop meaningful work. Write your present clarities and commitments as they relate to the key ideas in this book. Use the chapter titles to focus your thinking if you wish.

Reflect on where you experience energy for action to carry forward your clarities and commitments. Describe this in a separate statement.

When Diana did this, she was impressed with how far she had come. A lively woman in her mid-thirties, she holds a well paying position with Safeway. An accountant with excellent computer skills, she's the one who makes sure that everyone in her region is paid on time and that proper deductions are taken for each employee. "It's a great job — I know that," she exclaimed. "But I'm sick of spending so much time in front of the computer. I want to work more with people."

After using the processes described in this book, Diana wrote down some of her clarities and commitments as follows:

My Clarities and Commitments

The **Vocational Focus** I am exploring:
- *Human resource training in a large organization*

The **Gifts** I want to use:
- *Group facilitation*
- *Commitment to people's growth*
- *Knowledge of financial workings (a large organization)*

The **Meaning** I want to incorporate:
- *People who are empowered can empower others*

The **Parameters** that shape my work:
- *Make over $30,000*
- *Full-time*
- *Stay in Safeway system if possible*

The **People** who support my efforts . . . etc.

"I'm not in a new job yet," she says, "but when I line up my learnings like this, I can see that I've become clear and committed in a number of ways. I know I want to give at least a year to exploring a career switch to human resource training. That feels good! I am committed to developing and using the gifts I've identified. I know the kind of salary I need, and that clarity is energizing.

Things happened that we did not want: things we fought against to keep from happening, things that were painful and disruptive. But, once they happened, they brought unexpected opportunities.

Arnold Beisser
"Flying Without Wings"[2]

Confusion — Prelude to Creation

"Sure I know the kind of work I'd like, but I'm scared to do what it takes to get there," said Jaime, a participant in one of our seminars. "I'm a high school English teacher, and to do that well takes everything I have. It's so exhausting. I'd really love to give up teaching and earn a living with my art."

"Well, why don't you?" asked another seminar participant.

"It's taken me so long to get to where I am. I'm 35, have a nice apartment, a car. For the first time, I have a decent income and don't have to live on the margin. It's not easy to throw that away. On the other hand, I know if I keep this job, it will kill me. I am, frankly, just plain afraid to change. Where will I find the courage?"

Jaime knew what he wanted to do, something he could have been wholeheartedly working toward, but he was immobilized by fear, uncertainty, and doubt. The seminar participants came up with some interesting responses.

A retired person in his seventies said, "I find risk-taking to be an acquired skill. It takes practice. First, I take little risks, then larger ones. Slowly, my ability to risk is strengthened."

"Right now, my predominant feeling is uncertainty," responded a young editor who wanted to explore the possibility of doing something with dance in her life. "At this point, I'm taking dance and movement classes and letting myself flow with the uncertainty and that seems OK. I don't have to know the specifics yet."

"For me," said a lawyer, who was in the process of becoming a professional photographer/author, "it's been more like gradually easing into the shallow end of the pool as I'm ready. Slowly my hobby of traveling and photography, along with my appreciation of nature and sacred sites, gathered more and more strength. First the photographs I took began appearing in other people's books. Then a publisher advanced me money to produce my own text and photographs. Now I have the confidence that if I set off for a swim, the water will buoy me up."

Each of these people made different points about how to meet the unknown and move through the chaos of confusion to creation. The following is a review of their points with some additional ones included. They are offered as encouragement as you contemplate your next move.

- **Take a small risk at a time.** Sometimes the step you contemplate is just too big to start you off. Break it into several smaller ones.
- **Stay with the uncertainty.** Wait it out. This is a natural state of affairs and nothing to be too alarmed about. It will pass. It's a little like being in a sandstorm: Sometimes the best thing to do is fall down on the ground, wrap your robe about you, and wait until it's over. Eventually the force of the storm will subside.
- **Be open to help from others.** The forces of fear or uncertainty may be strong enough to push you outside yourself to seek another's advice or encouragement. That is positive. Feel good about asking others to help you sort through confusion.
- **Take apart the blockage.** A feeling of fear or confusion is like a rolling snowball. Negative possibilities stick to it as it gains speed. In short order you're saddled with an anxiety of unmanageable size. Put the brakes on. Split this fear into pieces. Name them. Decide one at a time how you will address each component.
- **Gradually build up the thing you love.** Perhaps Jaime's art skills are not strong enough to propel him into a new profession. This might give rise to his

hesitancy in making the switch. Like the lawyer, he needs to take it slow, strengthening these skills before diving into a career change.

- **Turn the blockage into a question.** Convert "I'm afraid" (blockage) into "How can I gain more courage to do what I want?"(question). Then live with the question, allowing the answers to unfold in their own time.
- **Develop the perspective of humor.** Ram Dass, when asked about his attitude toward inner fears replied, "In all the years of taking drugs, being a Freudian, being a therapist, meditating, having a guru, Sufi dancing, whatever, I haven't gotten rid of one neurosis yet. The only difference is that instead of these monsters, there are these little schmoos now, and I just invite them in for tea."[3]

The process of creating a new attitude toward work or a new work to do will feel blocked at times. It happens and is to be expected. The important thing is to find ways to get beyond it.

As you contemplate carrying out the statement of present clarities and commitments that you wrote in Segment 1, do any attitudes or feelings arise that cause you to feel immobilized? If yes, name them. Start from the point of view of blockage. Say, "I feel blocked by _____." "I'm afraid of _____."

Review the strategies described above for addressing these blocks. Choose and plan to carry out two that seem most appropriate at this time.

Describe in writing the strategies you want to use and how you will carry them out. For example, Lillian wrote:

Blockage
The job I want very much involves speaking in front of other people, but I feel blocked by my fear of public speaking.

Strategies to Address My Fear
1. Convert the blockage into a question: How can I develop the courage to speak in front of people?
2. Be open to help from others: I'm going to start asking people how they developed the skill of public speaking.

3

Write the vision down . . .
since this vision is for its own time only;
eager for its own fulfillment, it does not deceive;
if it comes slowly, wait,
for come it will, without fail.

Habakkuk 2:2,3[4]

Focus on the Future with the Present Well in Mind

When climbers scale a peak they are elated. Austrians might toast each other with a nip of schnapps, an American just might grin and say, "All right!" Their journey's purpose has been accomplished.

So, too, with this work of vocational exploration. Perhaps you have reached the destination toward which you were moving. You have identified what "working from the heart" means to you and have either found it or know where to look.

Or perhaps, with map in hand, you realize that although the

journey has yielded some clarity, the road to meaningful work still stretches before you.

If this is the case with you, you need to know how to proceed on your own. In *The Path of Least Resistance,* Robert Fritz describes a way to create next steps that are both appropriate and will take you where you want to go. He says that the most important question you can ask of yourself is "What do I want?" — or more precisely, "What result do I want to create?"[5] When you envision those results as if they are already a reality, power is unleashed to make them happen. This power to create results is, of course, tempered by current reality. But out of the tension between vision and reality, feasible and appropriate next steps manifest themselves. These steps, when taken, cause the vision and reality to change. You then can repeat the process, incorporating the new information you have gained.

This process is not new. You have already engaged in parts of it throughout this book. You have envisioned the meaning you want to incorporate, the gifts you want to use, the "people help" you need, the kind of work you want to do. You have looked at the reality of money you need to earn, the time you have to work, and the wishes of your loved ones related to your choices. And you have made action plans consisting of identifying people to interview, material to read, and hands-on experience to undertake.

What is fresh is Fritz's particular way of describing creative change. When you compare your vision with your current reality, you may feel discouraged. The discrepancy can cause anxiety, which is unproductive and will throw you off course. But it is this very tension produced by the difference between vision and reality that can give you power to move forward. When you realize that this tension is healthy and motivating, you can relax and allow next steps to occur to you that take both vision and reality into account. In other words, vision and reality are two sides of a fuller truth.

The ability to make constructive use of this tension for discovering next steps toward the result you want depends, according to Fritz, on your making a fundamental choice: You must choose "to be the predominant creative force in your own life."[6] This means that you will not allow other people or circumstances to assume this role for you. Yes, people and circumstances can influence you. But the responsibility for being the predominant creative force in your own life rests with you.

When Diana struggled to state her vision as if it were already happening, she found that the process did not come easily. And when she considered her current reality in terms of that vision, she felt discouraged. She wrote down her two descriptions as follows:

My Vision for Future Work

I am a skilled trainer at Safeway responsible for organizing and offering courses in team-building, productivity increase, and company benefits. This work makes me feel great. I feel like my gifts and creativity are used every day. Interaction with people, that's what I love, and seeing folks increase their skills. Requests for my services come in all the time — I'm busy, people need me. Consistent feedback tells me that employees and departments work better and feel better after taking my courses.

Reality

Currently my job requires monthly accounting and computer skills — things I know but no longer want to do. I've taken one course in training and loved it, but have no other formal preparation for a career in human resource development. The training division at Safeway is currently full. It does not need another person.

Diana attempted to see her vision and reality as two sides of a greater truth. She decided to let the two dialogue within herself for a while and allow next steps to surface in their own time.

President of the Philippines Corazin Aquino provides an impressive example of how this kind of dialogue ultimately works. What more horrifying circumstance to undergo than to witness your husband's assasination upon his return to Manila to lead the opposition party! Resisting the temptation to cave into immobilizing anxiety, she decided to stand for election herself.

Her first calling, or her initial vision of her own vocation, was to be a supportive wife to her husband, Ninoy Aquino, the strongest opponent of the incumbent President Ferdinand Marcos. During her husband's seven-year imprisonment, she was at his side as much as possible, keeping him informed of world events and family matters, and at the same time, being a liaison to his followers. Then came the reality of Ninoy's death and his followers' request for her to run for election. Immediate next steps occurred to her: consult with friends and advisors plus take some quiet time for retreat and meditation. Out of this came her conclusion and a recasting of her vision for her vocation: "We had to present somebody who was the complete opposite of Marcos, someone who has been a victim. Looking around, I may not be the worst victim, but I am the best known."[7]

As *Time* reported, "Soon the implausible turned into the improbable. Finally the improbable became the impossible. [A housewife-turned-politician] who had entered politics just two months earlier led a crusade against a canny and durable autocrat who had ruled for twenty years" and won by a landslide standing on a platform of "faith, hope and charity."[8]

Look over your Summary Pages and the work you did in Segments 1 and 2. Describe your vision of the work you want to do. Use the present tense — as though it were already happening. Describe it as fully as possible. Convey the positive feelings associated with doing what you really want to do.

Then describe current reality as you now experience it related to the work you want to do. Do not omit any part of your current reality that matters to you now.

When you have created your vision and reality statements, make a conscious choice to be the predominant creative force in your life. Rechoose the vision you have just described even as you are aware of your current reality. Create a symbol to express your vision and your feelings about it.

For now, rest with these activities. Let vision and current reality relate to each other for a period of time within the deeper reaches of your consciousness.

If you keep doing little things about it, your dream, which was amorphous at first, will begin to take shape, like a statue emerging from a chunk of marble.

Carolyn Jabs
"How to Kick a Dream Into Action"[9]

Bite-sized Chunks to Move You Forward

When Diana pondered what she wrote about vision and current reality, she remembered the course in training she had taken. "When I was learning and practicing those training skills, I felt super," she mused. "Everyone told me how well I did — but also how great I looked while I was in the course. One person even said he had never seen me so happy."

"I'd love to take more courses even if Safeway won't pay for them. And much as I'd want to stay at Safeway if I possibly could, I should begin to learn about other job possibilities in training." Once these thoughts had surfaced, Diana was ready to write down the following:

> **Next Steps**
>
> I will take additional courses in training on my own time to accomplish two goals:
>
> learn more
>
> find out about jobs that use these skills

The beauty of Fritz's process of describing vision, current reality, and next steps is that it focuses on a positive vision for the future. Too often, obstacles wield more influence than is appropriate. When you envision a future outcome that excites you, energy rises, and you can imagine steps toward that future which you want to take, bite-sized chunks that move you forward. This is a much livelier process than focusing on a present problem, positing a goal, and then planning next steps to achieve the goal and strategies to minimize the obstacles.

Fritz's process also helps you envision choices as life unfolds. In one of our seminars, Sandy took a ball and, rolling it forward, said, "This is the way my life is — it unfolds as it goes. I'm not a goal maker, but I do want to grow in my work." Fritz's process honors that feeling of evolution and combines it with "futuring" in a way that helps not only track progress but create it.

Review the vision and reality you described in Segment 3. Look again at the symbol you made to express your vision. Having allowed your vision and reality to interact with each other, now, as Diana did, list steps you could take to move you toward your vision.

It's important not to take for granted that we human beings can choose, can dream. We are living in a world with countless opportunities to create something which did not exist before. Celebration allows us to honor those human qualities of spirit that say "yes" to challenge, that lead us to create, no matter what the odds.

John Graham
"Celebrating Success"[10]

Celebrate Success and New Commitments

At their fortieth high school reunion, 58-year-olds mingle and recall old connections and recount current situations. Grandchildren and retirement plans are big topics. Don, the local middle school principal and city councilman, is asked how he likes his jobs. "I love them," he replies. "There's always a new challenge. I'm very happy I'm in this sort of work." Don had this type of upbeat attitude in high school and has maintained it all his life.

As you leave the nest and fly on your own, the questions to ask are: How do I keep the momentum going? How do I continue to take actions and cultivate attitudes that result in fulfilling, enjoyable work?

Two people who know a lot about keeping up momentum are John Graham and Anne Medlock. Founders of The Giraffe Project, whose aim is to inspire "people to stick their necks out for the common good," they recognize and celebrate people like Earl Zela Aldridge. Shocked by the explosion of a Jersey City chemical plant, Aldridge got himself appointed environmental inspector and put in "18-hour days, staking out dumpsites, collecting volumes of data and identifying 90 illegal dumps." Despite the opposition of the organizations who continue to dump, Aldridge continues his crusade to leave for the children of his town "the cleanest city of the world."[11]

John Graham and Anne Medlock operate The Giraffe Project on a shoestring, and often in the red. What keeps their spirits up?

"Celebrating every success," writes John. "Particularly those that may seem too small or insignificant to even recognize as 'successes' — like the letterhead coming back from the printer on time or the official you've been trying to get on the phone actually calling you back."[12]

Most of us are not used to congratulating ourselves as often as John and Anne recommend. Perhaps we're obsessed with scaling the peak and don't stop to affirm how well we packed our rucksack. When, however, we recognize steps taken toward our dream, when we acknowledge results achieved, however miniscule, we gain momentum for taking the next step and the next. "Each success seems to make the next one easier, and big successes seem to follow an appreciation of smaller ones," writes Graham. "Resources appear out of nowhere. Obstacles fall as if by magic. Celebration is a way to keep the dice hot, to keep the magic going. To switch metaphors, imagine that celebrating success is pump-priming — say thanks for every trickle and a real stream can follow."[13]

Yes, there may be mistakes, failures, fruitful opportunities missed along the way. None of us is omniscient — the way unfolds before us, and we can't avoid those times of going off course. The challenge is to recognize when we're veering away from our particular vision of work from the heart and to make a quick adjustment and recovery. As Robert Fritz says, "The art of creating is often found in your ability to adjust or correct what you have done so far."[14] In other words, create, adjust, create, adjust, create, adjust.

Fritz suggests that each recognition of failure can be the most important moment of our lives because it is then that we adjust the vision to correspond more closely with reality. John Graham echoes the same thought:

> . . . if things take a turn you didn't expect or plan for, accept the shifts as part of the creative process that was simply beyond your capacity to know at the time. Welcome it. Adjust the vision. Enjoy your flexibility and the results it can help you achieve.[15]

Realize that your future will contain failures as well as successes, both celebration and disappointment, times when sticking your neck out will bring results and times it will be ignored.

Now is the time to celebrate all the clarities and commitments you have, the specific ways you intend to take action to move your work life forward and the hopes you have for the future.

Look over your work from Segments 1, 2, 3, and 4. Describe where you hope to be in six months and in one year. Here is what Diana wrote:

Hopes

By next June I want to have enough information to decide whether I should stay with Safeway or put major effort into exploring other companies. I will also have taken one more training course.

By next January I want to decide whether a move from accounting to a career in training is realistic for me.

GATHERING

6

Purpose: *To affirm what has been accomplished and to complete the time together*
Leaders Bring: *candles and matches*
Everyone Bring:
Statement of clarities and commitments from Segment 1
Strategies to overcome blockages from Segment 2
Vision statement and symbol from Segment 3
Next steps from Segment 4
Hopes from Segment 5

Warm-Up (Everyone)   **30 minutes**

1. Place vision symbols in the center of your circle around a lit candle.
2. Take them in — ask each other about them. Have a laugh or two.
3. Read your vision statements to each other, holding a lighted candle as you do so.
4. Celebrate!

Recognition and Affirmation (Everyone)   40 minutes

1. Each person take a few minutes to review the work you brought to the Gathering. Prepare to share the parts of your final work that carry the most energy now.
2. When everyone is ready, give each person time to describe:
   - clarities and commitments (not all of them, just those you feel most energized by)
   - strategies to overcome blockages
   - next steps to move forward
   - hopes for where you want to be in six months and a year from now
3. Exchange feedback
4. Place your papers in the center of the group (or between partners) and celebrate work done with a round of applause/cheers.

Appreciation and Closing (Everyone)   20 minutes

1. Each person share how the group sessions have been for you. Include what you have appreciated and what you wish had been different, (i.e. ideas for improvement next time).
2. Close with encouraging words to each other as you take next steps on your own.
3. Read the following for a sendoff:

Be a Giraffe.

Stick your neck out for the common good.

Choose,

and continually choose

work that uses the best of you

to make the world a better place.

When you go off course,

adjust quickly.

And celebrate, celebrate, CELEBRATE

every success along the way!

I'm just back from this wonderful two week drama workshop I attended to celebrate my completion of the seminar. It capped off my work with you. It's something I've always wanted to do, and it felt great!

Seminar Participant

Keep Flying!

You've celebrated your work together with your group or your partner. Now the challenge is to keep the celebratory mood going as you move on without the committed structure of the Gathering sessions to spur you on. Here are some ideas:

- place your next steps on the Summary Page for this chapter and feel good about your plans
- take a well-earned rest for a while
- put some dates on the calendar to mark when you'll take your next steps
- plan a dinner out with your partner or group members to catch up after a month

Do one thing to give yourself the huge pat on the back you deserve for good work well done.

APPENDIX 1

Training Decisions

Some Factors To Consider

There are many valid reasons to get further training. Here are some of them:

1. **Academic knowledge.** You may want to gain academic grounding in a specific field of study such as urban planning, art therapy, or public relations. This could be done through taking one or two courses or perhaps a full-degree program.

2. **Skills.** Specific "how to" skills such as drafting, group process, accounting, low-income housing advocacy can be part of degree programs or often are given in separate workshops or programs.

3. **Credentialing.** Certain fields require specific types of training to enter at particular levels; this varies a great deal. It is important to find out what is required in your own field of interest and not assume that just because you have management training, for example, that you will be credentialed to work in all management positions.

4. **Affiliation.** You may want to be affiliated with a recognized center in the field of your interest. For example, conflict management is now taught in several universities; to complete one of these programs trains you in a recognized approach to that field.

5. **Contacts.** Sometimes it is important to meet people personally who are active in fields that interest you. One way is to take training in which they are involved as leaders or participants.

6. **Status and recognition.** A way to be accepted as competent and available in a field is to attend training offered by people with known reputations in that field. They can see your ability in action and can perhaps help you find the work you want to do.

7. **Discernment.** One way to decide whether a particular field is worth pursuing is to take some short-term training in that field and get a firsthand feel for it and the people involved before making a deeper commitment.

8. **Change and newness.** Sometimes a breath of fresh air is important. Taking some training in your own field or a related or even not-so-related field can make this happen — for example, movement, dance, marketing.

Practical Issues to Take Into Account

In deciding which is the best training for you, there are several issues to consider. Some are related to the reasons for training just mentioned. Which programs will offer what you want in the way of knowledge, skills, credentialing, affiliation, contacts, status, discernment, and newness? In addition, here are some other issues to consider:

1. **Money.** How much does the program cost? How much can I afford to invest in my own training in light of the return on my investment?
2. **Timing.** Does the length of program, time of day, time in the year fit my situation?
3. **Location.** Is the location convenient or attractive to me?
4. **Leadership.** Do the leaders have a good reputation? Can they offer me what I want in a way that is motivating?

Factors in Making a Wise Decision

The more care you take with your decision making, the better served you will be by your choice. Consider the following:

1. **Assess your needs.** Recognize what you need from training and why; try to do as much homework as possible on the best training alternatives for you.
2. **Talk with participants in the programs you are considering.** Be specific. Ask to see the books they read; discuss the labs and activities of the program; find out the pros and cons of that program from their perspective.
3. **Be aware of what training is valued by those with whom you may intend to work.** Ask for advice and suggestions from those who are supporting you in the field, that is, mentors, advisors.

4. **Interview the people who run the programs.** Remember that they usually want your business and may be prepared to be flexible, but it is up to you to be imaginative. Unnudged, the people in charge will usually go by the rules and approach things from the perspective of their program, not your unique vocation or experience. Here are some questions you might ask:
    a. What is the purpose of the program?
    b. How long does it take? How much time is involved?
    c. How much does it cost?
    d. What kinds of credentials will I obtain if I participate?
    e. What kinds of work might I expect to find if I go through your program?
    f. What kind of help do you provide for helping me find work?
    g. What are the components of your program?
        - lectures
        - lab
        - papers
        - practicum
        - student/teacher interaction
    h. Can you give me the names of some recent participants?
5. **Make a comparison chart of programs you are considering.** Talk options over with a friendly advisor.

Additional Points to Consider

1. **Training is a lifelong process.** There is no ultimate or perfect training experience at a particular time. Each has advantages and drawbacks.
2. **Some people seek universally understood qualifying training experiences.** Others (because of the nature of their field) recognize that there are no universally accepted training experiences. Some fields are more tightly regulated than others as far as training goes.

3. **Some training decisions cannot and should not be rushed.** It is better to get a period of less demanding training such as workshops and short-term events before entering a more demanding degree program.

4. **Sometimes a person wants to skip some steps in training.** Those who do not have a full undergraduate degree sometimes want to go right into a graduate-level program. This can be done in some instances, but it takes a good deal of preparation to make a strong case for such a move. Suggested ways to prepare:

   a. Find out formal requirements beforehand; do some investigating about the policy on flexibility.

   b. Talk about your situation with people who know that system; find out what they are looking for in a candidate, such as experience in the field, background reading and study, ability to handle the work load.

   c. Document your case in presentable form with emphasis on what program coordinators are looking for — that is, address these issues. For example, if an academic graduate department wants to know whether you can handle the course content intellectually, be prepared to say you have read and understood one or more of the texts used.

   d. Be prepared to negotiate. You might want to skip undergraduate work altogether, whereas the program might require one or two courses in psychology or philosophy. You might want to be a full-time student, but the program might recommend a lighter load, or accept you on probation, etc.

5. **It is important to trust your feelings and own sense of timing in making good training decisions.**

6. **Don't hesitate to ask for help in these decisions. They are hard.**

7. **One way to keep abreast of training opportunities is to get on the mailing lists of various training groups.** You can keep a running file of their offerings and consider how they meet your requirements for training.

8. **There are many different types of training, all of which have validity:**
   a. Self-study — working out your own program of reading and exposure to people and projects
   b. Continuing education programs
   c. Special skills training
   d. Degree programs
   e. Apprenticeship/internship

Writing Up Your Interview

When you write up your training interviews in your notebook or on cards, make sure that it is in a form that you can go back to and readily understand. Include:

> *Name of Program*   *Date of Interview*
> *Contact Person You Interviewed & Position*
> *Phone*
> *Address*
> *Summary of Learnings*

If you interview a participant in the program, incorporate that person's observations in your summary.

APPENDIX 2

Interviewing for Information

What It Is and How To Go About It

The term and technique called "interviewing for information" comes from the employment counseling field. If you are looking for work in a particular field, you do not get far by simply sending resumés to personnel offices. The best jobs are not always handled through personnel offices or advertised in newspapers. Like the best houses for sale that are snatched up before being listed, the best jobs are often learned about through inside contacts.

But what if you don't have "inside contacts"? Here is where interviewing for information comes in. Through people you know, you find out about individuals who work in the field you want to explore and make appointments to talk with them. You then ask these contacts to tell you what is going on in the field, what possible jobs may be opening up, and any other information useful to you in your search.

Interviewing for information is a well-known technique for fact-gathering related to a job search. What is not so widely known is its usefulness in many other areas of life. In a broad sense, interviewing for information can be defined as a formal technique for gathering information necessary for decision making.

When you do interviewing of this sort, it is important to be as clear as possible about what you hope to receive from the person you are meeting with. You should think through the kinds of concrete information you want: leads on jobs, other people who could help you, organizations or workshops that could be useful, books to read, conferences to attend, etc. Be sure you receive as much of that concrete information as you need.

Also be aware that your feelings may be "all over the place" before, during, and after these interviews. Your feelings are important indicators, so try to read the messages in them. If you don't like the person you are interviewing, why? If you feel let down, why? If you are excited, why? One natural feeling that may occur is a sense of being "less than" the person you interview because that person is in a more secure position than you are. Recognize that this happens, talk it over with a friend, but don't give more meaning to it than it deserves.

Interviewing for information is useful if done well, but can have negative effects if done poorly. That is why it is good to have a thorough knowledge of all the steps involved, as well as practice in using them. Then you can adapt the technique for informal use. Here are the steps that are involved:

Preparation

1. **Choose the person/organization to interview.** Start with someone who will be easy to approach — for example, a person you already know or someone a friend knows. Practice with those people and slowly move to people who present more of a challenge, such as someone you don't know or a person who is more experienced than you are.

2. **Find out as much as you can beforehand about the person/organization.** Consider obtaining descriptive material on the work or organization involved, or ask the person you will be meeting to send you printed information in advance of the interview.

3. **Establish the day and length of the interview.** Asking for an hour is appropriate.

4. **For your own clarity, prepare in writing a brief paragraph about yourself** (who you are and where you are in your search) **and the purpose of the interview** (why you have chosen this person and the kind of information or help you need). The written preparation can help you state clearly and succinctly over the phone why you're making the contact and what you hope to gain. It helps you avoid two common pitfalls: speaking too long about yourself or assuming the person knows about you and your purpose without being clearly told.

5. **Prepare your questions for this person.** Divide your questions into two parts:

a. Ask about the individual — his or her background, the why and how of this vocational choice, job duties, opinion about the good and negative points of the work, etc.

b. Ask the person for help with your situation — where you can get training, what kinds of job possibilities there are for your skills, etc. Work out a reasonable number of questions that can be dealt with in the allotted time and be conscious of forming them in a way that will elicit the specific information you need.

Execution

1. **Check the amount of time you have for the interview.**

2. **Go over in summary form what you want to cover and why.** Tell briefly who you are, where you are in your life, why you have chosen to talk with this person, what you hope to find out, and why you want to find it out. Perhaps go over in general form your line of questioning with some idea of timing. For example, "I have several questions to ask about you, your background, and your job experience. That should take about a half an hour. Then I'd like to use our last half hour to ask your advice and thoughts about some questions I have about my own direction." Consider showing the person your resumé if you have one in order to give a quick picture of your situation.

3. **If you want to tape the interview, this would be the time to ask.**

4. **Remember that you asked for the interview and you are in control of the time.** It is easy for the person being interviewed to linger on points that may not interest you. You must keep the person on track in appropriate ways. For example, "That is very helpful, but I would like more information about _____."

5. **Keep track of the time.** Five minutes before you are to end, start bringing the interview to a close. This is the time to ask the person if you can use his or her name in making other contacts. Do this only if it is appropriate.

6. **Thank the person and leave promptly.** If you feel you may want to see the person again or call later for additional clarification, ask if that would be possible.

Debriefing: What happened?

As soon as possible (perhaps before you go on to your next activity!), look at your notes and fill in points that you did not write down — pertinent facts or any feelings you have about the person, yourself, the content, the dynamics.

Evaluation: What did it mean?
1. **Identify what was positive and negative** about:
   - Your questions — did they elicit the information you needed?
   - Your conduct — is there anything you can improve?
   - The person, information, leads, ideas
   - What was pertinent, helpful, or motivating to you?
   - What do you need to discard?
   - Were negative feelings generated that might have a message for you - what is it?
2. **What is all this telling you about yourself?** What clues have you received personally from this interviewing process?

Follow-up
1. **Write a letter of thanks to the person.** In it you can include any information you promised to send, anything you wish the person to remember about you or what happened, and any word about follow-up you intend to do.
2. **Look over the notes of your interview and decide which leads you want to pursue or other ideas you want to build on.**
3. **Think through the big picture. Where do you go from here?** What next moves are suggested by your experience with the person?

Write-up
1. If you are on a serious search, it is helpful to yourself and to anyone helping you to **write in summary form a report of the interview.** This should include: the name, address, phone, and position of the person; the date of the interview; why you interviewed the person; a summary of what you learned; and

any evaluative comments that are useful to you and those helping you.

2. **If you don't do a summary, consider writing important data on a card for ready access.**

Interviewing for information is a challenge to do well. Once you have learned how to do it in a formal way, you will find that you can use it informally in many situations. It is an art. You will always be learning how to do it more effectively.

BIBLIOGRAPHY

A list of the books we've found most useful over the years

Anzalone, Joan (editor). *Good Works: A Guide to Careers in Social Change.* New York: December, 1985.
> Profiles of individuals working for social change, plus a listing of relevant organizations and resources.

Berkowitz, Bill. *Local Heroes.* Lexington, Massachusetts: Lexington, 1987.
> Portraits of 20 people who have made a difference in grass roots America. If they can do it, so can we!

Brody, Jean Lisette. *Mid-life Careers.* Philadelphia: Westminster Press, 1983.
> Special emphasis on career change. Practical, anecdotal style.

Campbell, David. *If You Don't Know Where You're Going, You'll Probably End Up Somewhere Else.* Allen, Texas: Argus Communications, 1974.
> Written especially for young people, this helps you raise and address the big questions of what to do in life and how to find help.

Catalyst. *Resume Preparation Manual: A Step by Step Guide for Women.* New York: Catalyst, 1978.
> A particularly helpful guide for women re-entering the job market.

May, Rollo. *The Courage to Create.* New York: Bantam, 1975.
> A brief but powerful discussion of creativity — how it works, how it feels, how to cultivate this "healthiest impulse."

McMakin, Jacqueline with Rhoda Nary. *Doorways to Christian Growth.* San Francisco: Harper & Row, 1984.
> A faith perspective on discovering gifts and life purpose. A practical approach, including acitivites to do alone and with others.

Miller, Luree. *Late Bloom.* New York: Paddington Press, 1979.
> Stories of how women have changed their lives, careers, and relationships, a celebration of those who also have decided to "live according to their talents."

Moran, Peg. *Invest in Yourself.* Garden City, New York: Doubleday, 1983.
> How to start your own business plus interviews with 13 people who have done it.

Parker, Yana. *Damn Good Resumé Guide.* Berkeley, California: Ten Speed Press, 1989.
> Our most used resumé guide. Great on one-page resumés. We would not be without it.

Phifer, Paul. *College Majors and Careers: A Resource for Effective Life Planning.* Garrett Park, Maryland: Garrett Park, 1987.
> A handy directory that lists fields of interest, related occupations, relevant avocational and leisure-time activities, related skills, sources for further exploration.

Robbins, Lois. *Waking Up in the Age of Creativity.* Santa Fe, New Mexico: Bear and Company, 1985.
> Specific practical ways to free up and foster creativity in all aspects of life.

NOTES

INTRODUCTION

1. Studs Terkel, WORKING: PEOPLE TALK ABOUT WHAT THEY DO ALL DAY AND HOW THEY FEEL ABOUT WHAT THEY DO (New York: Pantheon Books, a Division of Random House, Inc., 1974), xxix.

1. DOING WHAT YOU LOVE (Gifts)

1. Paula Ripple, GROWING STRONG AT BROKEN PLACES (Notre Dame, IN: Ave Maria Press, 1986), 63.
2. Stephen M. Holloway & Harvey A. Hornstein, "How Good News Makes Us Good," *Psychology Today*, December 1976, 76-108.
3. Joan Smith Rideout, "Our Gifts: Joy and Responsibility," from a sermon given at Shrewsbury Community Church, Shrewsbury, VT.
4. Bill Moyers, A WORLD OF IDEAS (Garden City, NY: Doubleday, 1989), 159.
5. Elizabeth O'Connor, EIGHTH DAY OF CREATION: GIFTS AND CREATIVITY (Dallas: WORD, Inc., 1971), 40.
6. *Ibid.*, 19.
7. Joseph Campbell with Bill Moyers, THE POWER OF MYTH (New York: Doubleday, 1988), 151.
8. *Ibid.*, 118.
9. *Ibid.*, 155.
10. Mary R. Schramm, GIFTS OF GRACE: DISCOVERING AND USING YOUR UNIQUE ABILITIES (Minneapolis: Augsburg Publishing House, 1982), 62.

2. WHAT'S IT ALL ABOUT? (Meaning)

1. Quoted by Judy Mann, "The Quest for Life's Meaning," *The Washington Post Magazine*, 14 June 1985.
2. John Graham, "Can Giraffes Survive in the Jungle?" *The Giraffe Gazette*, Vol. V., No. 1 (Winter 1989), 11.
3. Pete Earley, "Desmond Tutu: God and the Politics of Commitment," *The Washington Post Magazine*, 16 February 1986, 8.
4. Brita L. Gill-Austern, "Awakening the Trusting Heart," *Keeping You Posted* (New York: Office of Communication, United Church of Christ). Vol. 20, No. 7 (September 1985), 2.
5. Earley, "Desmond Tutu," 9-10.
6. Russell Schweickart, "No Frames, No Boundaries." In William P. Marsh, editor, *Earth's Answer* (New York: Lindisfarne Press, 1987), 11-12.

7. Marilyn Ferguson, THE AQUARIAN CONSPIRACY (Los Angeles.: J. P. Tarcher, Inc., 1980), 342.

8. Rita Reynolds-Gibbs & Paula Underwood Spencer, "A Teacher's Guide to WHO SPEAKS FOR WOLF" (Austin, TX: The Meredith Slobod Crist Memorial Fund, 1983), 3.

9. Mary Caroline Richards, CENTERING: IN POTTERY, POETRY, AND THE PERSON (Middletown, CT: Wesleyan University Press, 1964), 13.

3. LET'S GET PRACTICAL (Parameters)

1. Norman Boucher & Laura Tennen, "In Search of Fulfillment," *New Age Journal*, May 1985, 27.

2. Ellen Goodman, CLOSE TO HOME (New York: Simon & Schuster, Inc., 1979), 158-159.

3. Carolyn Jabs, "How to Kick a Dream into Action," *Self*, May 1986, 122.

4. *Rom. 7:15.* From NEW TESTAMENT IN MODERN ENGLISH, REVISED EDITION by J. B. Phillips (New York: MacMillan Publishing Company, 1958).

5. Elizabeth O'Connor, OUR MANY SELVES (New York: Harper & Row, Publishers, Inc., 1971).

6. Gail Sheehy, PATHFINDERS (New York: Bantam Books, 1982), 125.

4. CHOOSE AND EXPLORE (Vocational Focus)

1. Rollo May, THE COURAGE TO CREATE (New York: W. W. Norton & Company, Inc. 1975), 67.

2. Brenda Ueland, IF YOU WANT TO WRITE (1938; reprint ed., St. Paul, MN: Graywolf Press, 1987), 64, 114.

3. Frank Barron, "Creativity: The Human Resource," a pamphlet accompanying an exhibition researched and designed by The Burdick Group with the cooperation of the California Academy of Sciences through a grant from the Chevron Family of Companies, 1979, 5.

4. Barbara Sher with Annie Gottlieb, WISHCRAFT: HOW TO GET WHAT YOU REALLY WANT (New York: Viking Penguin Inc., 1979), 152.

5. Richard Nelson Bolles, THE THREE BOXES OF LIFE AND HOW TO GET OUT OF THEM (Berkeley, CA: Ten Speed Press, 1981), 84.

6. Quoted by Charlotte Painter, GIFTS OF AGE: PORTRAITS AND ESSAYS OF 32 REMARKABLE WOMEN (San Francisco: Chronicle Books, 1985), 146.

7. Gail Sheehy, PATHFINDERS (New York: Bantam Books, 1982), 120.

5. CALL IN REINFORCEMENTS (Companionship)

1. Natasha Josefowitz, PATHS TO POWER (Reading, MA: Addison-Wesley Publishing Company, 1980), 93.
2. Carla Hall, "For Father Hartke, A Fitting Farewell," *The Washington Post Magazine*, 26 February 1986.
3. From a letter to the Reverend Phillips Brooks, dated June 8, 1891. Courtesy of the American Foundation for the Blind, New York, NY.
4. Alice Walker, IN SEARCH OF OUR MOTHERS' GARDENS (New York: Harcourt Brace Jovanovich, 1983), xviii.
5. Joseph Campbell with Bill Moyers, THE POWER OF MYTH (New York: Doubleday, 1988), 120.
6. Eva Jessye as quoted by Brian Lanker in I DREAM A WORLD: PORTRAITS OF BLACK WOMEN WHO CHANGED AMERICA (New York: Stewart, Tabori & Chang, 1989), 20.
7. Dorothee Sölle, "For My Young Comrades." In OF WAR AND LOVE (Maryknoll, NY: Orbis Books, 1975), 143.
8. Colman McCarthy, INNER COMPANIONS (Washington, D.C.: Acropolis Books, Ltd. 1975), 18.
9. Carol Van Sickle, "Jobless at 61: A Success Story," *Ms.*, October 1986, 68.
10. John Naisbitt, MEGATRENDS: TEN DIRECTIONS TRANSFORMING OUR LIVES (New York: Warner Books, 1982), 192.

6. FEED THE WHOLE PERSON (Spiritual Nourishment)

1. Theodore Roszak, WHERE THE WASTELAND ENDS (Winchester, MA: Faber & Faber, Inc., 1972), xxii.
2. Madeleine L'Engle, THE IRRATIONAL SEASON (New York: The Seabury Press, 1977).
3. Joseph Campbell with Bill Moyers, THE POWER OF MYTH (New York: Doubleday, 1988), 92.
4. Natalie Curtis, THE INDIAN'S BOOK (1907; new ed., New York: Dover Publications, 1968), 11.
5. James Fowler & Sam Keen, LIFE MAPS: CONVERSATIONS ON THE JOURNEY OF FAITH (Dallas: WORD, Inc., 1978), 120.
6. Marilyn Ferguson, THE AQUARIAN CONSPIRACY (Los Angeles: J. P. Tarcher, Inc., 1980), 379.
7. Thomas Ryan, WELLNESS, SPIRITUALITY, AND SPORTS (Mahwah, NJ: Paulist Press, 1986), 38.

7. CONSIDER YOUR ENVIRONMENT (Work Environment)

1. Marvin R. Weisbord, PRODUCTIVE WORKPLACES (San Francisco: Jossey-Bass, 1987), 1.
2. John Naisbitt & Patricia Aburdene, RE-INVENTING THE CORPORATION (New York: Warner, 1985), 22.
3. Thomas Peters & Robert Waterman, IN SEARCH OF EXCELLENCE (New York: Harper and Row, 1982), xxiii.
4. Naisbitt & Aburdene, RE-INVENTING THE CORPORATION, 21.
5. Levering, Moskowitz & Katz, 100 BEST COMPANIES TO WORK FOR IN AMERICA (Reading, MA: Addison-Wesley Publishing Co., Inc., 1984), xiii.
6. Daniel V. Biles, III, "Pursuing Excellence in Ministry," *Action Information,* Alban Institute (Washington, D.C.), Vol. XIV, No. 2 (March/April 1988), 4.
7. Robert Levering & Milton Moskowitz, A GREAT PLACE TO WORK: WHAT MAKES SOME EMPLOYERS SO GOOD AND MOST SO BAD (New York: Random House, 1988), 221. The rights to the original "you done GOOD" award form are owned by Tektronix, Inc.
8. John Naisbitt, MEGATRENDS: TEN NEW DIRECTIONS TRANSFORMING OUR LIVES (New York: Warner, 1982), 95.
9. Naisbitt & Aburdene, RE-INVENTING THE CORPORATION, 24.
10. Anne Truitt, DAYBOOK: THE JOURNAL OF AN ARTIST (New York: Pantheon Books, 1982), 93.
11. Weisbord, PRODUCTIVE WORKPLACES, 265-266.
12. Mary Caroline Richards, CENTERING: IN POTTERY, POETRY, AND THE PERSON (Middletown, CT: Wesleyan University Press, 1962), 92.

8. WHAT'S NEXT? (Next Move)

1. Studs Terkel, WORKING: PEOPLE TALK ABOUT WHAT THEY DO ALL DAY AND HOW THEY FEEL ABOUT WHAT THEY DO (New York: Pantheon Books, a Division of Random House, Inc., 1974), xv.
2. Arnold Beisser, FLYING WITHOUT WINGS, (Garden City, NY: Doubleday, 1987), 27.
3. Ram Dass, "Is Enlightenment Good for Your Mental Health?" *The Common Boundary,* Vol. 6, Issue 5 (September/October 1988), 8.
4. *Hab. 2:2,3.* From THE JERUSALEM BIBLE, READER'S EDITION, edited by Alexander Jones (Garden City, NY: Doubleday, 1968).
5. Robert Fritz, THE PATH OF LEAST RESISTANCE: LEARNING TO BECOME THE CREATIVE FORCE IN YOUR OWN LIFE (New York: Fawcett Columbine, 1989), 133, 163.
6. *Ibid.,* 193

7. Robert Fritz, "Cory," *TIME Magazine*, 5 January 1987, 26.

8. *Ibid.*, 21.

9. Carolyn Jabs, "How to Kick a Dream into Action," *Self*, May 1986, 122.

10. John Graham, "Celebrating Success" *The Giraffe Gazette*, Vol. IV, No. 4 (Summer/Fall 1988), 12.

11. *Ibid.*, 9.

12. *Ibid.*, 12.

13. *Ibid.*, 12-13.

14. Fritz, THE PATH OF LEAST RESISTANCE, 53

15. Graham, "Celebrating Success," 13.

CREDITS

Grateful acknowledgment is made to the following copyright holders for permission to use their copyrighted material:

Acropolis Books, Ltd., for the quotation from INNER COMPANIONS by Colman McCarthy, Washington, D.C. Copyright 1975.

Addison-Wesley Publishing Co., Inc., for the following quotations:
From THE 100 BEST COMPANIES TO WORK FOR IN AMERICA by Levering/Moskowitz/Katz. Copyright © 1984. Reprinted by permission of Addison-Wesley Publishing Co., Inc., Reading, MA.

From PATHS TO POWER by Natasha Josefowitz. Copyright © 1980. Reprinted by permission of Addison-Wesley Publishing Co., Inc., Reading, MA.

The Alban Institute, Inc., for the quotation from "Pursuing Excellence in Ministry," by Daniel V. Biles, III. Reprinted by permission from The Alban Institute, Inc., 4125 Nebraska Avenue, NW, Washington, D.C. 20016. Copyright 1988. All rights reserved.

American Foundation for the Blind for the quotation from a letter to the Reverend Phillips Brooks, June 8, 1891.

Augsburg Fortress, Publishers, for the quotation from GIFTS OF GRACE: DISCOVERING AND USING YOUR UNIQUE ABILITIES by Mary R. Schramm. Copyright © 1982 Augsburg Publishing House. Reprinted by permission.

Ave Maria Press, for the excerpt from GROWING STRONG AT BROKEN PLACES by Paula Ripple. Copyright © 1986 by Ave Maria Press, Notre Dame, IN 46556. All rights reserved. Used with permission of the publisher.

Bantam, Doubleday, Dell Publishing Group, Inc., for the following excerpts:
From THE JERUSALEM BIBLE, copyright © 1966 by Darton, Longman & Todd, Ltd. and Doubleday, a division of Bantam, Doubleday, Dell Publishing Group, Inc. Reprinted by permission.

From PATHFINDERS by Gail Sheehy. Copyright © 1982 by Gail Sheehy. Reprinted by permission of Bantam Books, a division of Bantam, Doubleday, Dell Publishing Group, Inc.

Frank Barron, for the quotation from the pamphlet, "Creativity The Human Resource," by Frank Barron, Aptos, California, 1979.

Common Boundary Magazine, for the quotation stated by Ram Dass from COMMON BOUNDARY MAGAZINE, Vol. 6, Issue 5, September/October, 1988.

The Meredith Slobod Crist Memorial Fund, for the quotation from A Teacher's Guide to WHO SPEAKS FOR WOOLF by Rita Reynolds-Gibbs & Paula Underwood Spencer. Copyright 1983 by Paula Underwood Spencer.

Doubleday, for the following excerpts:

From FLYING WITHOUT WINGS, by Arnold Beisser. Copyright © 1987 by Arnold Beisser. Used by permission of Doubleday, a division of Bantam, Doubleday, Dell Publishing Group, Inc.

From THE POWER OF MYTH by Joseph Campbell with Phill Moyers. Copyright © 1988 by Alfred Van Der Marck and 'S Productions. Reprinted by permission of Doubleday, a division of Bantam, Doubleday, Dell Publishing Group, Inc.

From A WORLD OF IDEAS, Bill Moyers, Editor Betty Sue Flowers. Copyright © 1989 by Public Affairs Television, Inc. Reprinted by permission of Doubleday, a division of Bantam, Doubleday, Dell Publishing Group, Inc.

Dover Publications, for the quotations from THE INDIAN'S BOOK by Natalie Curtis. Copyright 1968 by Dover Publications. Used by permission.

Fawcett Columbine, for the quotations from THE PATH OF THE LEAST RESISTANCE: LEARNING TO BECOME THE CREATIVE FORCE IN YOUR OWN LIFE by Robert Fritz. Copyright 1989. Used by permission of Fawcett Columbine.

The Giraffe Gazette, for the quotations from John Graham of The Giraffe Project in THE GIRAFFE GAZETTE, Vol. IV, No. 4, Summer/Fall, 1988; Vol. V, No. 1, Winter 1989.

Graywolf Press, for the quotations from IF YOU WANT TO WRITE by Brenda Ueland. Copyright © 1987 by the Estate of Brenda Ueland. Reprinted by permission of Graywolf Press.

Harcourt Brace Jovanovich, Inc. for the excerpt from IN SEARCH OF OUR MOTHERS' GARDENS by Alice Walker. Copyright © 1983 by Alice Walker. Reprinted by permission of Harcourt Brace Jovanovich, Inc.

Harper and Row, for the quotation from IN SEARCH OF EXCELLENCE by Thomas Peters and Robert Waterman. Copyright 1982. Reprinted by permission.

Jossey-Bass, Inc., for the quotations from PRODUCTIVE WORKPLACES by Marvin R. Weisbord. Copyright 1987 by Marvin R. Weisbord. Reprinted by permission of Jossey-Bass, Inc. and Marvin R. Weisbord.

Carolyn Jabs, for the quotations from the article, "How to Kick a Dream into Action," which first appeared in SELF, May, 1986.

Lindisfarne Press, for the quotation from the article, "No Frames, No Boundaries," by Russell Schweickart in EARTH'S ANSWER, William P. Marsh, editor. Lindisfarne Press, 1987.

Macmillan Publishing Company, for the quotation from NEW TESTAMENT IN MODERN ENGLISH, REVISED EDITION by J. B. Phillips. Copyright © 1958, 1960, 1972 by J. B. Phillips. Reprinted by permission of Macmillan Publishing Company.

MS Magazine for the quotation from the article, "Jobless at 61: A Success Story," by Carol Van Sickle. MS MAGAZINE, October, 1986.

New Age Journal, for the quotation from the article, "In Search of Fulfillment," by Norman Boucher and Laura Tennen. NEW AGE JOURNAL, May 1985.

W. W. Norton & Company, Inc., for the quotation from COURAGE TO CREATE by Rollo May. Copyright 1975. Reprinted by permission of W. W. Norton & Company, Inc.

Orbis Books, for the quotation from OF WAR AND LOVE by Dorothee Sölle. Copyright 1975. Reprinted by permission of Orbis Books.

Pantheon Books, for the following exerpts:
From DAY BOOK: JOURNAL OF AN ARTIST by Anne Truitt. Copyright 1982 by Anne Truitt, Reprinted by permission of Pantheon Books, a division of Random House, Inc.

From WORKING: PEOPLE TALK ABOUT WHAT THEY DO ALL DAY AND HOW THEY FEEL ABOUT WHAT THEY DO by Studs Terkel. Copyright 1974. Reprinted by permission of Pantheon Books, a division of Random House, Inc.

Paulist Press, for the quotation from WELLNESS, SPIRITUALITY, AND SPORTS by Thomas Ryan. Copyright 1986. Reprinted by permission of Paulist Press.

Psychology Today for the quotation from the article, "How Good News Makes Good," by Stephen M. Halloway & Harvey A. Hornstein. PSYCHOLOGY TODAY, December, 1976.

Random House, Inc., for the quotation from A GREAT PLACE TO WORK: WHAT MAKES SOME EMPLOYERS SO GOOD AND MOST SO BAD by Robert Levering and Milton Moskowitz. Copyright 1988 by Robert Levering. Reprinted by permission of Random House, Inc.

Dr. Theodore Roszak, for the quotation from WHERE THE WASTELAND ENDS. Copyright 1972 by Dr. Theodore Roszak. Used by permission.

Joan Smith Rideout, M.Ed., for the excerpt from sermon, Shrewbury Community Church, Shrewbury, Vermont. Used by permission of Joan Smith Rideout, M.Ed., 299 South Union Street, Burlington, Vermont.

Simon & Schuster, Inc., for the selection from CLOSE TO HOME by Ellen Goodman. Copyright ©1979 by The Washington Post. Reprinted by permission of Simon & Schuster, Inc.

St. Martin's Press, Inc., for the quotation from THE AQUARIAN CONSPIRACY by Marilyn Ferguson. Copyright 1980 by Jeremy P. Tarcher, Inc., Los Angeles. Reprinted by permission of St. Martin's Press, Inc.

Stewart, Tabori & Chang, for the quotation of Eve Jessye, as quoted in I DREAM A WORLD by Brian Lanker, edited by Barbara Summers. Copyright 1989 by Stewart, Tabori & Chang, New York.

Tektronix, Inc., for the "you done GOOD" award. Used by permission.

INDEX

About the Authors

Jacqueline McMakin and **Sonya Dyer** met 25 years ago doing interracial work in the Washington, D.C. area, and ever since have sought together to overcome barriers and open closed doors for themselves and others.

Sparked by a commitment to create new ways to live and work and to pass on the tools that had been useful to them in vocational development, they established the nonprofit Lay Ministry Project. At first based in the church, their work later expanded to include people not necessarily rooted in a faith tradition but eager to explore the role of meaning in their lives and its expression through work. Their approach emphasizes the importance of people helping each other find what they are looking for. It offers a combination of career development, psychological, and spiritual tools to help people articulate life direction and develop a vocation that honors the totality of their lives.

In addition to her work with Sonya, Jackie with Rhoda Nary created a collaborative effort called Doorways, which offers training and consultation to help churches mentor the spiritual and vocational development of members. She and Rhoda are the authors of *Doorways to Christian Growth* (Harper & Row, 1984).

Sonya is the leader of the pastoral team of the Seekers Community, Church of the Saviour, Washington, D.C., and through For Love of Children (FLOC), works directly with urban homeless families.

Sonya is a trained social worker. Jackie holds an M.A. degree in Theology from The Catholic University of America.

Sonya and Jackie are eager to hear about your experience with *Working from the Heart.* If you start a group, please let them know. They would like to know where these groups are happening, how they are going, and any useful feedback you might have for future editions. Reach them at: 1309 Merchant Lane, McLean, VA 22101.

LuraMedia PUBLICATIONS

by Marjory Zoet Bankson
BRAIDED STREAMS
Esther and a Woman's Way
of Growing
(ISBN 0-931055-05-09)

SEASONS OF FRIENDSHIP
Naomi and Ruth
as a Pattern
(ISBN 0-931055-41-5)

by Alla Renée Bozarth
WOMANPRIEST
A Personal Odyssey
(ISBN 0-931055-51-2)

by Lura Jane Geiger
ASTONISH ME, YAHWEH!
Leader's Guide
(ISBN 0-931055-02-4)

by Lura Jane Geiger
and Patricia Backman
BRAIDED STREAMS
Leader's Guide
(ISBN 0-931055-09-1)

by Lura Jane Geiger, Sandy Landstedt,
Mary Geckeler, and Peggy Oury
ASTONISH ME, YAHWEH!
A Bible Workbook-Journal
(ISBN 0-931055-01-6)

by Kenneth L. Gibble
THE GROACHER FILE
A Satirical Exposé of
Detours to Faith
(ISBN 0-931055-55-5)

by Ronna Fay Jevne, Ph.D.
and Alexander Levitan, M.D.
NO TIME FOR NONSENSE
Self-Help for the Seriously Ill
(ISBN 0-931055-63-6)

by Ted Loder
EAVESDROPPING ON THE ECHOES
Voices from the Old Testament
(ISBN 0-931055-42-3 HB)
(ISBN 0-931055-58-X PB)

GUERRILLAS OF GRACE
Prayers for the Battle
(ISBN 0-931055-01-6)

NO ONE BUT US
Personal Reflections on
Public Sanctuary
(ISBN 0-931055-08-3)

TRACKS IN THE STRAW
Tales Spun from the Manger
(ISBN 0-931055-06-7)

by Jacqueline McMakin
with Sonya Dyer
WORKING FROM THE HEART
For Those Who Hunger for Meaning
and Satisfaction in Their Work
(ISBN 0-931055-65-2)

by Elizabeth O'Connor
SEARCH FOR SILENCE
Revised Edition
(ISBN 0-931055-07-5)

by Donna Schaper
BOOK OF COMMON POWER
Narratives Against the Current
(ISBN 0-931055-67-9)

by Renita Weems
JUST A SISTER AWAY
A Womanist Vision of Women's
Relationships in the Bible
(ISBN 0-931055-52-0)

LuraMedia is a company that searches for ways to encourage personal growth, shares the excitement of creative integrity, and believes in the power of faith to change lives.